Life in the
United Kingdom Test

Citizenship Study Guide

Paul Lancaster and Mary-Ann Coull

Published by Lancaster and Coull Publishers

Lancaster and Coull Publishers
11 Milton Close
Horton
Berkshire
SL3 9PP United Kingdom

Email (for orders and customer services enquiries):
orders@lancasterandcoull.co.uk
Visit our home page on: www.lancasterandcoull.co.uk

ISBN: 978-0-9554853-0-5

Printing History:
April 2007   First Edition

Printed and bound in England by Biddles

TABLE OF CONTENTS

INTRODUCTION

About this book

This book and CD-ROM aims to help you study for your Life in the UK test.

After each chapter you will find a QuickStudy section that includes a short summary of important facts contained in the chapter. These summaries are included as a guide and do not represent the content of the questions that will be asked. Ensure you read and study all the material in each chapter carefully.

At the end of the book there is a glossary to help you understand key words and their meanings and an index with the relevant page number to help you refer back to the chapter.

About the CD

Included at the back of this book is a useful CD containing practice test questions to test your knowledge. Each time you run the quiz you will get 24 random questions from an extensive database of questions and answers. Practice until you are confident of your answers.

The practice questions will not be exactly the same in the actual test. They are meant to represent the sort of questions that the test contains.

By studying the relevant chapters in this book, following the Study Program and using the practice test quiz software, we are confident that you will be well on the way to passing your test with ease.

Remember, there is no substitute for study and revision.

We hope you will find our study guides useful and would love to hear your success story. May we wish you the very best with your test!

Chapter 1 — ABOUT THE TEST

Becoming a British Citizen

Becoming a British citizen is an important event in your life and is something that you can feel proud of.

Britain is a country where people of many different cultures and faiths live. What brings British people together is that they listen to different points of view, they have respect for equal rights and they believe that community is important.

Becoming a British citizen means you will have:

- the right to a British passport
- the right to vote in national elections
- the opportunity to play an active role in your community and wider society

As an individual, you also have many talents and experiences to bring to UK society.

Being a British citizen doesn't mean you have to lose your own identity. There will, however, be things about life in the UK that you should know about before you become a citizen.

That's why the Life in the UK Test has been introduced. Studying for and taking the test will give you the practical knowledge you need to live in this country and to take part in society.

Introducing the test

If you are applying for naturalisation as a British citizen or for indefinite leave to remain, you will need to show that you know about life in the UK. If you live in England, Scotland, Wales or Northern Ireland, you can do this in two ways: by taking the Life in the UK Test or by taking combined English for Speakers of Other Languages (ESOL) and citizenship classes.

You should take the test if you are applying for naturalisation as a British citizen and your level of English is ESOL Entry 3 or above. If your level of English is lower than ESOL Entry 3 and you wish to apply for naturalisation, you will need to attend combined English language (ESOL) and citizenship classes instead.

ESOL and citizenship classes help you to improve your English and learn more about life in the UK. You can take these classes at your local further education or community college. To find out more about ESOL and citizenship classes, contact your local college, or call the Life in the UK Test Helpline on 0800 015 4245.

If you are not sure what your level of English is, work through the tutorial at http://www.lifeintheuktest.gov.uk or contact your local further education college or Learndirect centre can give you an initial assessment. If you need help finding somewhere near you to take an initial assessment, then call the Life in the UK Test Helpline on 0800 015 4245.

If you need help with finding a test centre, call the Life in the UK Test Helpline on 0800 015 4245 or visit http://www.lifeintheuktest.gov.uk.

At present, the test is only available in English, but will be offered in Welsh and Scottish Gaelic in the future. The test will not be made available in any other languages.

You should take the test before you apply for naturalisation as a British citizen, provided you meet all the other requirements for naturalisation. The Home Office website http://www.ind.homeoffice.gov.uk/applying/nationality/ provides more information on how to apply for naturalisation as a British citizen.

If you pass the test, you are given a letter which proves you have been successful. This is called your pass notification letter. You will need to attach your pass notification letter to your filled-in citizenship application form and send both to the Home Office. The Home Office will retain the information it gets from test centres for a reasonable period. However, you should submit your application as soon as possible after taking the test.

You take the test on a computer in an official test centre. It's designed to be very easy to use. Help is available at your local UK online centre if you've never used a computer before. Computer access at your local UK Online centre is free, and friendly staff are always there to help you. For more information about UK Online visit http://www.ufi.com/ukol/.

Preparing for the test

The test contains 24 questions on Life in the United Kingdom and will last for 45 minutes. It's based on chapters 2, 3, 4, 5 and 6 of this book.

This book also contains a practice test quiz CD-ROM (attached to the back of the book) containing individual quizzes for each chapter. The quizzes are taken from a comprehensive question and answer database. Also available is a quiz using all the questions from all the chapters.

The layout of the test

This is an example of what the Home Office Life in the UK Test looks like.

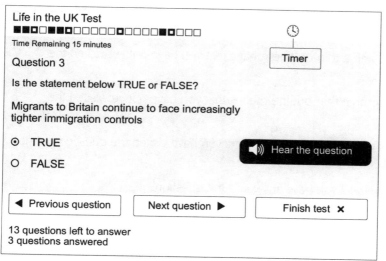

The **timer** counts down the time from when you start the test. It is always there, so you know how much time you have left. Halfway through the test time, you will get a time alert. You will get two more time alerts: **ten** and **two** minutes before the test ends.

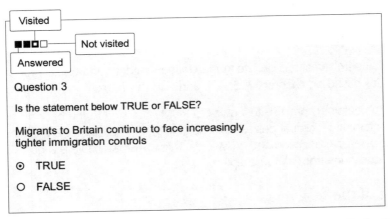

The **boxes along the top** let you move between questions. Each of the 24 boxes represents one question. You can move quickly to any question by simply selecting a box with your mouse or a keyboard shortcut.

A **white box** with a **thin outline** means that you have not yet visited the question.

A **white box** with a **thin outline** means that you have not yet visited the question.

A **white box** with a **bold outline** means you have visited the question but not answered it.

A **solid box** means you have answered the question.

Navigation around the test

Using the boxes to move around the test lets you visit questions first and return to them later. This is especially useful when you're not sure what the answer to a question is, or if you want to change a previous answer.

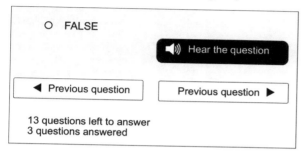

Questions left to answer tells you how many questions you have left to answer.

Questions answered tells you how many you have answered.

Keyboard shortcuts

There are some keyboard shortcuts available which you can use to answer questions in the test. You may use the keyboard shortcuts or a mouse, whatever you feel more comfortable with.

Answering questions
To select the 1st answer, press the number 1.
To select the 2nd answer, press the number 2.
To select the 3rd answer, press the number 3.
To select the 4th answer, press the number 4.
To deselect an answer, press the relevant number key again.

Other shortcuts

To move to the next question, press the letter N.
To move to the previous question, press the letter P.

To hear the question, press the letter H.

To finish the test, press the letter F.

Types of questions

The test contains four different types of question. The examples here aren't real test questions, but they show you how the real test works.

The first type of question involves selecting ONE correct answer from FOUR options.

> When were immigrants from the West Indies
> invited to come to the United Kingdom?
>
> O   1946
>
> O   1947
>
> O   1948
>
> O   1949

Radio buttons deselect automatically when you select another answer.

Your selected answer will have a white area around it and a dot in the circle.

The next type of question involves deciding whether a statement is TRUE or FALSE.

> Is the statement below TRUE or FALSE?
>
> Migrants to Britain continue to face increasingly
> tighter immigration controls
>
> ⊙   TRUE
>
> O   FALSE

Your selected answer will have a white area around it and a dot in the circle.

The third question type involves selecting **TWO** correct answers from **FOUR** options.

> Which TWO crimes are associated with wanting money for drugs?
>
> ☐ Burglary
>
> ☐ Mugging
>
> ☐ Kidnapping
>
> ☐ Car theft

You should not select more or fewer answers than this. You need to select a tick box again to deselect it.

Your selected answers will have white areas around them and ticks in the boxes.

The last question type involves selecting which **ONE** of **TWO** statements you think is correct.

> To become a local councillor, a candidate must have?
>
> ◉ A local connection with the area
>
> ○ Lived in the area for at least 10 years

Your selected answer will have a white area around it and a dot in the circle.

Selecting answers

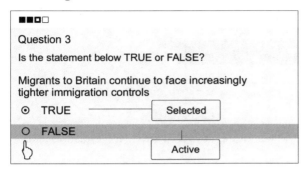

When you move to an answer, the area around it turns grey. This means the answer is active and you can select it. If you are using a mouse, your pointer arrow will also change to a pointer finger.

Once you select an answer, the area around it turns white. If you have selected a radio button, a dot will also appear in the circle.

Usability preferences

The test is available in a range of other formats to help candidates with particular usability preferences.

You can choose to take your test in these formats:

Large font – large font on a standard test background

High contrast – large black font on a cream background

High visibility – large yellow font on a black background.

Tell your centre about any usability preferences you have when you book your test.

Ending the test

The **Finish test** button ends the test or the keyboard shortcut F ends the test.

You select **Finish test** when you have completed all 24 questions. If you run out of time, your test will end automatically. You will **NOT** be allowed to finish your current question.

Don't worry if you select **Finish test** by mistake; you will be asked to confirm your decision. Remember: none of your answers are final until you select **Finish test** and confirm your decision. Your test results will **NOT** be displayed on screen at the end of the test.

After the test

After your test, the test supervisor will tell you whether or not you have passed.

You will be able to do a practice test at your test centre before you take the actual test.

If you don't pass the test the first time, you can redo it when you feel ready. There's no limit to the number of times you can take the test. Remember that you will be charged a fee each time you take the test.

Taking the test

When you arrive at the test centre, the test supervisor will ask for your full name, date of birth, nationality, country and place of birth, and your postcode. Your photographic ID will be checked and you will have to pay for your test (unless you have paid for it previously).

The test supervisor will check to make sure you have completed the prepare for the test section at http://www.lifeintheuktest.gov.uk/textsite/prepare_10.html.

It is important to go through this section of the website before you take the test.

You will then be logged on to a computer and will have time to complete a practice test on your computer before you begin the Life in the UK Test. The test supervisor will tell you when to begin your test and how long you have to complete it.

The test has a time limit of 45 minutes. This will give you plenty of time to choose your answers and check them again before the end. You do not need to rush to finish the test quickly. Remember to use all of the time that you are given. If you have certain medical conditions, you may be allowed more time.

You will find out your results when the test session has finished. The test supervisor will tell you whether or not you have passed. They will not tell you your pass mark.

The pass mark for the test is 75%.

If you pass the test, your test supervisor will give you a pass notification letter. This letter contains details of your test date, supervisor, centre location and a unique ID number. When you have filled in your citizenship application, you should attach your pass notification letter and send both to the Home Office. Your test centre will also send proof of your test results to the Home Office.

Your pass notification letter is very important: you should keep it in a safe place until you are ready to fill in your citizenship application. If you lose this letter, you will not be given a new one to replace it. The letter does not have an expiry date.

Your test supervisor will advise you if you have failed the test. You should not make an application for naturalisation as a British citizen if this happens.

You can take the test again, but we do not recommend that you do this straight away. You should go back and study chapters 2, 3, 4, 5 and 6 of this book and do the exercises contained in this book until you feel confident.

Your results notification letter will give you feedback on which areas of the handbook you need to look at again. You will then need to book a new test date and time with your test centre.

You should consider taking combined English language (ESOL) and citizenship classes at your local further education college before taking the test again.

Chapter 2 — A CHANGING SOCIETY

Migration to Britain

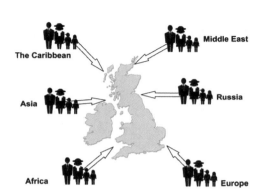

Many people living in Britain today have their origins in other countries. They can trace their roots to regions throughout the world such as Europe, the Middle East, Africa, Asia and the Caribbean. In the distant past, invaders came to Britain, seized land and stayed. More recently, people come to Britain to find safety, jobs and a better life.

Britain is proud of its tradition of offering safety to people who are escaping persecution and hardship. For example, in the 16th and 18th centuries, Huguenots (French Protestants) came to Britain to escape religious persecution in France. In the mid-1840s there was a terrible famine in Ireland and many Irish people migrated to Britain. Many Irish men became labourers and helped to build canals and railways across Britain.

From 1880 to 1910, a large number of Jewish people came to Britain to escape racist attacks (called 'pogroms') in what was then called the Russian Empire and from the countries now called Poland, Ukraine and Belarus.

Migration since 1945

After the Second World War (1939-45), there was a huge task of rebuilding Britain. There were not enough people to do the work, so the British government encouraged workers from Ireland and other parts of Europe to come to the UK to help with the reconstruction. In 1948, people from the West Indies were also invited to come and work

During the 1950s, there was still a shortage of labour in the UK. The UK encouraged immigration in the 1950s for economic reasons and many industries advertised for workers from overseas. For example, centres were set up in the West Indies to recruit people to drive buses. Textile and engineering firms from the north of England and the Midlands sent agents to India and Pakistan to find workers. For about 25 years, people from the West Indies, India, Pakistan, and later Bangladesh, travelled to work and settle in Britain.

The number of people migrating from these areas fell in the late 1960s because the government passed new laws to restrict immigration to Britain, although immigrants from 'old' Commonwealth countries such as Australia, New Zealand and Canada did not have to face such strict controls. During this time, however, Britain did admit 28,000 people of Indian origin who had been forced to leave Uganda and 22,000 refugees from South East Asia.

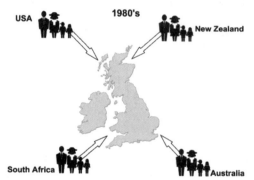

In the 1980s the largest immigrant groups came from the United States, Australia, South Africa, and New Zealand. In the early 1990s, groups of people from the former Soviet Union came to Britain looking for a new and safer way of life. Since 1994 there has been a global rise in mass migration for both political and economic reasons.

The changing role of women

In 19th-century Britain, families were usually large and in many poorer homes men, women and children all contributed towards the family income. Although they made an important economic contribution, women in Britain had fewer rights than men. Until 1857, a married woman had no right to divorce her husband. Until 1882, when a woman got married, her earnings, property and money automatically belonged to her husband.

In the late 19th and early 20th centuries, an increasing number of women campaigned and demonstrated for greater rights and, in particular, the right to vote. They became known as 'Suffragettes'. These protests decreased during the First World War because women joined in the war effort and therefore did a much greater variety of work than they had before. When the First World War ended in 1918, women over the age of 30 were only given the right to vote and to stand for election to Parliament. It was not until 1928 that women won the right to vote at 21, at the same age as men.

Despite these improvements, women still faced discrimination in the workplace. For example, it was quite common for employers to ask women to leave their jobs when they got married. Many jobs were closed to women and it was difficult for women to enter universities. During the 1960s and 1970s there was increasing pressure from women for equal rights. Parliament passed new laws giving women the right to equal pay and prohibiting employers from discriminating against women because of their sex. (see also chapter 6).

Women in Britain today

Women with children of school age

■ In work - almost 3/4 in paid work

■ Not in work

Women in Britain today make up 51% of the population and 45% of the workforce. These days girls leave school, on average, with better qualifications than boys and there are now more women than men at university.

Employment opportunities for women are now much greater than they were in the past. Although women continue to be employed in traditional female areas such as healthcare, teaching, secretarial and retail work, there is strong evidence that attitudes are changing, and women are now active in a much wider range of work than before. Research shows that very few people today believe that women in Britain should stay at home and not go out to work. Today, almost three-quarters of women with school-age children are in paid work.

In most households, women continue to have the main responsibility for childcare and housework. There is evidence that there is now greater equality in homes and that more men are taking some responsibility for raising the family and doing housework. Despite this progress, many people believe that more needs to be done to achieve greater equality for women. There are still examples of discrimination against women, particularly in the workplace, despite the laws that exist to prevent it. Women still do not always have the same access to promotion and better-paid jobs. The average hourly pay rate for women is 20% less than for men, and after leaving university most women still earn less than men.

Children, family and young people

In the UK, there are almost 15 million children and young people up to the age of 19. This is almost one-quarter of the UK population.

Over the last 20 years, family patterns in Britain have been transformed because of changing attitudes towards divorce and separation. Today, 65% of children live with both birth parents, almost 25% live in lone-parent families, and 10% live within a stepfamily. Most children in Britain receive weekly pocket money from their parents and many get extra money for doing jobs around the house.

Children in the UK do not play outside the home as much as they did in the past. Part of the reason for this is increased home entertainment such as television, videos and computers. There is also increased concern for children safety and there are many stories in newspapers about child molestation by strangers, but there is no evidence that this kind of danger is increasing.

Young people have different identities, interests and fashions to older people. Many young people move away from their family home when they become adults but this varies from one community to another.

Education

The law states that children between the ages of 5 and 16 must attend school. The tests that pupils take are very important and in England and Scotland children take national tests in English, mathematics and science when they are 7, 11 and 14 years old. (In Wales, teachers assess children's progress when they are 7 and 11 and they take a national test at the age of 14). The tests give important information about children's progress and achievement, the subjects they are doing well in and the areas where they need extra help.

Most young people take the General Certificate of Secondary Education (GCSE), or, in Scotland, Scottish Qualifications Authority (SQA) Standard Grade examinations when they are 16. At 17 and 18, many take vocational qualifications, General Certificates of Education attain Advanced level (AGCEs), AS level units or Higher/Advanced Higher Grades in Scotland. Schools and colleges will expect good GCSE or SQA Standard Grade results before allowing a student to enrol on an AGCE or Scottish Higher/Advanced Higher course.

AS levels are Advanced Subsidiary qualifications gained by completing three AS units. Three AS units are considered as one-half of an AGCE. In the second part of the course, three more AS units can be studied to complete the AGCE qualification.

Many people refer to AGCEs by the old name of A levels. AGCEs are the traditional route for entry to higher education courses, but many higher education students enter with different kinds of qualifications.

One in three young people now go on to higher education at college or university. Some young people defer their university entrance for a year and take a gap year. This year out of education often includes voluntary work and travel overseas. Some young people work to earn and save money to pay for their university fees and living expenses.

One in three young people move onto higher education

People over 16 years of age may also choose to study at Colleges of Further Education or Adult Education Centres. There is a wide range of academic and vocational courses available as well as courses which develop leisure interests and skills. Contact your local college for details.

Work

It is common for young people to have a part-time job while they are still at school. It is thought there are 2 million children at work at any one time. The most common jobs are newspaper delivery and work in supermarkets and newsagents. Many parents believe that part-time work helps children to become more independent as well as providing them (and sometimes their families) with extra income.

There are laws about the age when children can take up paid work (usually not before 14), the type of work they can do and the number of hours they can work (see www.worksmart.org.uk for more information).

It is very important to note that there are concerns for the safety of children who work illegally or who are not properly supervised and the employment of children is strictly controlled by law.

Health hazards

Many parents worry that their children may misuse drugs and addictive substances.

Smoking:
Although cigarette smoking has fallen in the adult population, more young people are smoking, and more girls smoke than boys. By law, it is illegal to sell tobacco products to anyone under 16 years old. In some areas, smoking in public buildings and work environments is not allowed.

Alcohol:
Young people under the age of 18 are not allowed to buy alcohol in Britain, but there is concern about the age some young people start drinking alcohol and the amount of alcohol they drink at one time, known as binge drinking It is illegal to be drunk in public and there are now more penalties to help control this problem, including on-the-spot fines.

Illegal drugs:
As in most countries, it is illegal to possess drugs such as heroin, cocaine, ecstasy, amphetamines and cannabis. Current statistics show that half of all

young adults, and about a third of the population as a whole, have used illegal drugs at one time or another.

There is a strong link between the use of hard drugs (e.g. crack cocaine and heroin) and crime, and also hard drugs and mental illness. The misuse of drugs has a huge social and financial cost for the country. This is a serious issue and British society needs to find an effective way of dealing with the problem.

Young people's political and social attitudes

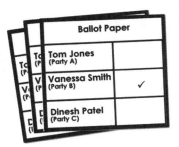

Young people in Britain can vote in elections from the age of 18. In the 2001 general election, however only 1 in 5 first-time voters used their vote. There has been a great debate over the reasons for this. Some researchers think that one reason is that young people are not interested in the political process.

Although most young people show little interest in party politics, there is strong evidence that many are interested in specific political issues such as the environment and cruelty to animals.

In 2003 a survey of young people in England and Wales showed that they believe the five most important issues in Britain were crime, drugs, war/terrorism, racism and health. The same survey asked young people about their participation in political and community events. They found that 86% of young people had taken part in some form of community event over the past year, and 50% had taken part in fund-raising or collecting money for charity. Similar results have been found in surveys in Scotland and Northern Ireland. Many children first get involved in these activities while at school where they study Citizenship as part of the National Curriculum.

Notes

Historical reasons for immigration to the UK

- In the distant past, invaders came to Britain, seized land and stayed.
- In the 16th and 18th centuries, Huguenots came to Britain to escape religious persecution.
- In the mid 1840s many Irish people migrated to Britain to escape a terrible famine in Ireland.
- Between 1880 and 1910, a large number of Jewish people came to Britain to escape racist attacks.

Immigration to the UK since 1945

- The British government encouraged workers from Ireland and other parts of Europe to come to the UK to help with the reconstruction after the Second World War.
- People from the West Indies were also invited to come and work.
- During the 1950s, Textile firms from the north of England and engineering firms from the Midlands brought workers from India and Pakistan.
- In the 1970's, 28,000 refugees of Indian origin came from Uganda and 22,000 refugees came from South East Asia.
- In the 1980s the largest immigrant groups came from the United States, Australia, South Africa, and New Zealand.
- In the early 1990's, groups of people came from the former Soviet Union.

Women's rights

- In 1918, women over the age of 30 were given the right to vote and to stand for election to Parliament.
- In 1928 the voting age for women was lowered to 21.
- Laws have been introduced to prevent discrimination against women in

the workplace.

Family

- Over the last 20 years, attitudes towards divorce and separation have changed.
- 65% of children live with both birth parents.
- Almost 25% live in lone-parent families.
- 10% live within a stepfamily.

Children and young people

- Most children in Britain receive weekly pocket money from their parents.
- Many get extra money for doing jobs around the house.
- Many young people move away from their family home when they become adults but this varies from one community to another.

Education

- Education Britain is free.
- It is compulsory for children between the ages of 5 and 16 years old.
- England and Scotland have compulsory testing at ages 7, 11 and 14.
- Wales assess children at 7 and 11.
- At 16, children can take GCSE's or vocational exams.
- At 17 and 18 they can take Advanced level exams.
- The government target is that half of all young people attend higher education.

Work

- There are strict laws about the age when children can take up paid work (usually not before 14), the type of work they can do and the number of hours they can work.

Health

- By law, it is illegal to sell tobacco products to anyone under 16 years old.
- Young people under the age of 18 are not allowed to buy alcohol.
- The misuse of drugs is a serious issue.

Politics

- Young people in Britain can vote in elections from the age of 18.

Notes

Chapter 3 — UK TODAY: A PROFILE

Population

In 2005 the population of the United Kingdom was just under 60 million people.

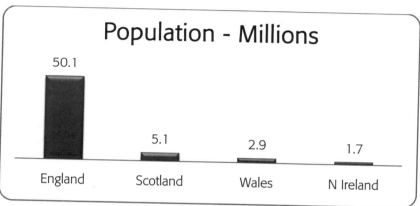

Population - Millions

50.1	5.1	2.9	1.7
England	Scotland	Wales	N Ireland

UK population 2005

		million
England	(84% of the population)	50.1
Scotland	(8% of the population)	5.1
Wales	(5% of the population)	2.9
N. Ireland	(3% of the population)	1.7
Total UK		59.8

Source: National Statistics

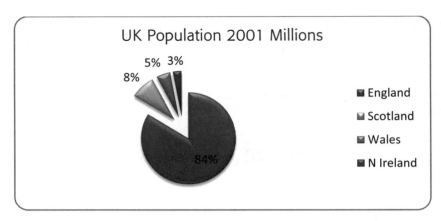

UK Population 2001 Millions

5% 3%

8%

84%

- England
- Scotland
- Wales
- N Ireland

The population has grown by 7.7% since 1971, and growth has been faster in more recent years. Although the general population in the UK has increased in the last 20 years, in some areas such as the North-East and North-West of England there has been a decline.

Both the birth rate and the death rate are falling and as a result the UK now has an ageing population. For instance, there are more people over 60 than children under 16. There is also a record number of people aged 85 and over.

The census

A census is a count of the whole population. It also collects statistics on topics such as age, place of birth, occupation, ethnicity, housing, health, and marital status.

A census has been taken every ten years since 1801, except during the second World War. The next census will take place in 2011.

During a census, a form is delivered to every household in the country. This form asks for detailed information about each member of the household and must be completed by law. The information remains confidential and anonymous; it can only be released to the public after 100 years, when many people researching their family history find it very useful. General census information is used to identify population trends and to help planning. More information about the census, the census form and statistics from previous censuses can be found at www.statistics.gov.uk/census

Ethnic diversity

The UK population is ethnically diverse and is changing rapidly, especially in large cities such as London, so it is not always easy to get an exact picture of the ethnic origin of all the population from census statistics. Each of the four countries of the UK (England, Wales, Scotland and Northern Ireland) has different customs, attitudes and histories.

People of Indian, Pakistani, Chinese, Black Caribbean, Black African, Bangladeshi and mixed ethnic descent make up 8.3% of the UK population. Today about half the members of these communities were born in the United Kingdom.

There are also considerable numbers of people resident in the UK who are of Irish, Italian, Greek and Turkish Cypriot, Polish, Australian, Canadian, New Zealand and American descent. Large numbers have also arrived since 2004 from the new East European member states of the European Union. These groups are not identified separately in the census statistics in the following table.

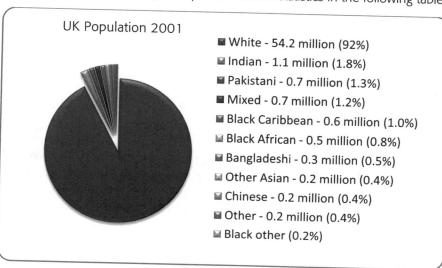

UK Population 2001

- White - 54.2 million (92%)
- Indian - 1.1 million (1.8%)
- Pakistani - 0.7 million (1.3%)
- Mixed - 0.7 million (1.2%)
- Black Caribbean - 0.6 million (1.0%)
- Black African - 0.5 million (0.8%)
- Bangladeshi - 0.3 million (0.5%)
- Other Asian - 0.2 million (0.4%)
- Chinese - 0.2 million (0.4%)
- Other - 0.2 million (0.4%)
- Black other (0.2%)

UK population 2001

	Million	UK Population %
White (including people of European, Australian, American descent)	54.2	92
Mixed	0.7	1.2
Asian or Asian British		
Indian	1.1	1.8
Pakistani	0.7	1.3
Bangladeshi	0.3	0.5
Other Asian	0.2	0.4
Black or Black British		
Black Caribbean	0.6	1.0
Black African	0.5	0.8
Black other	0.1	0.2
Chinese	0.2	0.4
Other	0.2	0.4

Source: National Statistics from the 2001 census

Where do the largest ethnic minority groups live?

The figures from the 2001 census show that most members of the large ethnic minority groups in the UK live in England, where they make up 9% of the total population. 45% of all ethnic minority people live in the London area, where they form nearly one-third of the population (29%). Other areas of England with large ethnic minority populations are the West Midlands, the South East, the North West, and Yorkshire and Humberside.

Proportion of ethnic minority groups in the countries of the UK

England	9%	Wales	2%
Scotland	2%	Northern Ireland	less than 1%

The nations and regions of the UK

The UK is a medium-sized country. The longest distance on the mainland, from John O'Groats on the north coast of Scotland to Lands End in the south-west corner of England, is about 870 miles (approximately 1,400 kilometres). Most of the population live in towns and cities.

There are many variations in culture and language in the different parts of the United Kingdom. This is seen in differences in architecture, in some local customs, in types of food, and especially in language. The English language has many accents and dialects. These are a clear indication of regional differences in the UK. Well-known dialects in England are Geordie (Tyneside), Scouse (Liverpool) and Cockney (London). Many other languages in addition to English are spoken in the UK, especially in multicultural cities.

In Wales, Scotland and Northern Ireland, people speak different varieties and dialects of English. In Wales, too, an increasing number of people speak Welsh, which is taught in schools and universities. In Scotland Gaelic is spoken in some parts of the Highlands and Islands and in Northern Ireland a few people speak Irish Gaelic Some of the dialects of English spoken in Scotland show the influence of the old Scottish language, Scots. One of the dialects spoken in Northern Ireland is called Ulster Scots.

Religion

Although the UK is historically a Christian society, everyone has the legal right to practise the religion of their choice. In the 2001 census, just over 75% said they had a religion: 7 out of 10 of these were Christians. There were also a considerable number of people who followed other religions. Although many people in the UK said they held religious belief, currently only around 10% of the population attend religious services. More people attend services in Scotland and Northern Ireland than in England and Wales. In London the number of people who attend religious services is increasing.

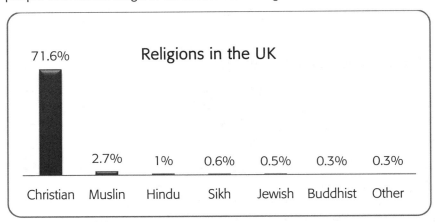

Religions in the UK	%
Christian (10% of whom are Roman Catholic)	71.6
Muslim	2.7
Hindu	1.0
Sikh	0.6
Jewish	0.5
Buddhist	0.3
Other	0.3
Total All	77
No religion	15.5
Not stated	7.3

Source: National Statistics from the 2001 census

The Christian Churches

In England there is a constitutional link between church and state. The official church of the state is the Church of England. The Church of England is called the Anglican Church in other countries and the Episcopal Church in Scotland and in the USA. The Church of England is a Protestant church and has existed since the Reformation in the 1530s. The king or queen (the monarch) is the head, or Supreme Governor, of the Church of England. The monarch is not allowed to marry anyone who is not Protestant. The spiritual leader of the Church of England is the Archbishop of Canterbury. The monarch has the right to select the Archbishop and other senior church officials, but usually the choice is made by the Prime Minister and a committee appointed by the Church. Several Church of England bishops sit in the House of Lords (see chapter 4). In Scotland, the established church is the Presbyterian Church; its head is the Chief Moderator. There is no established church in Wales or in Northern Ireland.

Other Protestant Christian groups in the UK are Baptists, Presbyterians, Methodists and Quakers. 10% of Christians are Roman Catholic (40% in Northern Ireland).

Patron saints

England, Scotland, Wales and Northern Ireland each have a national saint called a patron saint. Each saint has a feast day. In the past these were celebrated as holy days when many people had a day off work. Today these are not public holidays except for 17 March in Northern Ireland.

Patron saints' days

St David's day, Wales	1 March
St Patrick's day, Northern Ireland	17 March
St George's day, England	23 April
St Andrew's day, Scotland	30 November

There are also four public holidays a year called Bank Holidays. These are of no religious or national significance.

Customs and traditions

Festivals

Throughout the year there are festivals of art, music and culture, such as the Notting Hill Carnival in west London and the Edinburgh Festival. Customs and traditions from various religions, such as Eid ul-Fitr (Muslim), Diwali (Hindu) and Hanukkah (Jewish) are widely recognised in the UK. Children learn about these at school. The main Christian festivals are Christmas and Easter. There are also celebrations of non-religious traditions such as New Year.

The main Christian festivals

Christmas Day

25 December, celebrates the birth of Jesus Christ. It is a public holiday. Many Christians go to church on Christmas Eve (24 December) or on Christmas Day itself. Christmas is also usually celebrated by people who are not Christian. People usually spend the day at home and eat a special meal, which often includes turkey. They give each other gifts, send each other cards and decorate their houses. Many people decorate a tree. Christmas is a special time for children. Very young children believe that an old man, Father Christmas (or Santa Claus), brings them presents during the night. He is always shown in pictures with a long white beard, dressed in red. Boxing Day, 26 December is the day after Christmas. It is a public holiday.

Other festivals and traditions

New Year

1 January, is a public holiday. People usually celebrate on the night of 31 December. In Scotland, 31 December is called Hogmanay and 2 January is also

a public holiday. In Scotland Hogmanay is a bigger holiday for some people than Christmas.

Valentine's Day
14 February, is when lovers exchange cards and gifts. Sometimes people send anonymous cards to someone they secretly admire.

April Fools Day
1 April, is a day when people play jokes on each other until midday. Often TV and newspapers carry stories intended to deceive credulous viewers and readers.

Mother's Day
The Sunday three weeks before Easter is a day when children send cards or buy gifts for their mothers. Easter is also an important Christian festival.

Hallowe'en
31 October, is a very ancient festival. Young people will often dress up in frightening costumes to play 'trick or treat'. Giving them sweets or chocolates might stop them playing a trick on you. Sometimes people carry lanterns made out of pumpkins with a candle inside.

Guy Fawkes Night
5 November, is an occasion when people in Great Britain set off fireworks at home or in special displays. The origin of this celebration was an event in 1605, when a group of Catholics led by Guy Fawkes failed in their plan to kill the Protestant king with a bomb in the Houses of Parliament.

Remembrance Day
11 November, commemorates those who died fighting in World War 1, World War 2 and other wars.

Many people wear poppies (a red flower) in memory of those who died. At 11 a.m. there is a two-minute silence.

Sport

Sport of all kinds plays an important part in many people lives. Football, tennis, rugby and cricket are very popular sports in the UK. There are no United Kingdom teams for football and rugby. England, Scotland, Wales and Northern Ireland have their own teams. Important sporting events include, the Grand National horse race, the Football Association (FA) cup final (and equivalents in Northern Ireland, Scotland and Wales), the Open golf championship and the Wimbledon tennis tournament.

Chapter 3 — QuickStudy

Population

- In 2005, the population of the United Kingdom was just under 60 million people, the population of England was 50.1 million, the population of Scotland was 5.1 million, the population of Wales was 2.9 million and the population of N. Ireland was 1.7 million.

Census

- A census is a count of the whole population, It also collects statistics on topics such as age, place of birth, occupation, ethnicity, housing, health, and marital status.
- A census has been taken every ten years since 1801, except during the second World War.
- The next census will take place in 2011.

Ethnic diversity

- The largest ethnic minority UK are people of Indian descent, followed by people of Pakistani, Black Caribbean, Black African and then Bangladeshi descent of which about half were born in the United Kingdom.
- Most members of ethnic minority groups live in England, around 45% in the London area.
- Other areas of England with large ethnic minority populations are the West Midlands, the South East the North West and Yorkshire and Humberside.

Regions

- Welsh is spoken by an increasing number of people in Wales and the language is taught in schools and universities.
- Gaelic is spoken in some parts of the Highlands and Islands of Scotland and some of the dialects of English spoken in Scotland show

the influence of the old Scottish language, Scots.

- One of the dialects spoken in Northern Ireland is called Ulster Scots.
- Well-known dialects in England are Geordie (Tyneside), Scouse (Liverpool) and Cockney (London).
- The different regions in Britain are identifiable by differences in architecture, local customs, types of food, accent and dialect.

Religion

- The UK is historically a Christian society with 71.6% stating that they were Christians.
- 2.7% are Muslim, 1.0% are Hindu, 0.6% are Sikh, 0.5 are Jewish and 0.3% are Buddhist, with 0.3% stating that they had no recognised religion.
- Everyone in the UK has the legal right to practise the religion of their choice.
- The official church of the state (the established church), is the Church of England, which is called the Anglican Church in other countries and the Episcopal Church in Scotland and in the USA.
- The king or queen (the monarch) is the head, or Supreme Governor, of the Church of England.
- In Scotland, the established church is the Presbyterian Church; its head is the Chief Moderator.
- There is no established church in Wales or in Northern Ireland.

Patron saints

- The UK has 4 patron saints days. In Wales it is St David's day on March 1st, in Northern Ireland it is St Patrick's day on March 17th, in England it is St George's day on April 23rd and in Scotland it is St Andrew's day on November 30th.

Customs and traditions

- There are four public holidays a year called Bank Holidays. They are

January 1st, Spring Bank Holiday in May, Summer bank Holiday in August and Boxing Day on December 26th.

- The UK has further public holidays celebrating important Christian festivals.
- Christmas Day and Easter
- There are other festival days traditional days, such as Valentine's day, April Fool's day, Mothering Sunday, Hallowe'en, Guy Fawkes Night and Remberance Day.
- Customs and traditions from various religions, such as Eid ul-Fitr (Muslim), Diwali (Hindu) and Hanukkah (Jewish) are taught to children in school and are widely recognised in the UK.

Sports

- Football, tennis, rugby and cricket are very popular sports in the UK.
- Many people also play golf and follow horse racing.

Notes

Chapter 4 — HOW THE UNITED KINGDOM IS GOVERNED

The British Constitution

As a constitutional democracy, the United Kingdom is governed by a wide range of institutions, many of which provide checks on each others' powers. Most of these institutions are of long standing: they include the monarchy, Parliament (consisting of the House of Commons and the House of Lords), the office of Prime Minister, the Cabinet, the judiciary, the police, the civil service, and the institutions of local government. More recently, devolved administrations have been set up for Scotland, Wales and Northern Ireland. Together, these formal institutions, laws and conventions form the British Constitution. Some people would argue that the roles of other less formal institutions, such as the media and pressure groups, should also be seen as part of the Constitution.

The British Constitution is not written down in any single document as are the constitutions of many other countries. This is mainly because the United Kingdom has never had a lasting revolution, like America or France, so our most important institutions have been in existence for hundreds of years. Some people believe that there should be a single document, but others believe that an unwritten constitution allows more scope for institutions to adapt to meet changing circumstances and public expectations.

The Monarchy

Queen Elizabeth II is the Head of State of the United Kingdom. She is also the monarch or Head of State for many countries in the Commonwealth. The UK, like Denmark, the Netherlands, Norway, Spain and Sweden, has a constitutional monarchy. This means that the king or queen does not rule the country, but appoints the government which the people have chosen in democratic elections. Although the queen or king can advise, warn and encourage the Prime

Minister, the decisions on government policies are made by the Prime Minister and Cabinet.

The Queen has reigned since her father's death in 1952. Prince Charles, the Prince of Wales, her oldest son, is the heir to the throne.

The Queen has important ceremonial roles such as the opening of the new parliamentary session each year. On this occasion the Queen makes a speech that summarises the government's policies for the year ahead.

Government

The system of government in the United Kingdom is a parliamentary democracy. The UK is divided into 646 parliamentary constituencies and at least every five years voters in each constituency elect their Member of Parliament (MP) in a general election. All of the elected MPs form the House of Commons. Most MPs belong to a political party and the party with the largest number of MPs forms the government.

The law that requires new elections to Parliament to be held at least every five years is so fundamental that no government has sought to change it. A Bill to change it is the only one to which the House of Lords must give its consent. Some people argue that the power of Parliament is lessened because of the obligation on the United Kingdom to accept the rules of the European Union and the judgments of the European Court, but it was Parliament itself which created these obligations.

The House of Commons

 The House of Commons is the more important of the two chambers in Parliament and its members are democratically elected. Nowadays the Prime Minister and almost all the members of the Cabinet are members of the House of Commons. The members of the House of Commons are called 'Members of Parliament' or MPs for short. Each MP represents a parliamentary constituency, or area of the country: there are 646 of these. MPs have a number of different responsibilities. They represent everyone in their constituency, they help to create new laws, they scrutinise and comment on what the government is doing, and they debate important national issues.

Elections

There must be a general election to elect MPs at least every five years, though they may be held sooner if the Prime Minister so decides. If an MP dies or resigns, there will be another election, called a by-election, in his or her constituency. MPs are elected through a system called 'first past the post'. In each constituency, the candidate who gets the most votes is elected. The government is then formed by the party which wins the majority of constituencies.

The Whips

The Whips are a small group of MPs appointed by their party leaders. They are responsible for discipline in their party and making sure MPs attend the House of Commons to vote. The Chief Whip often attends Cabinet or Shadow Cabinet meetings and arranges the schedule of proceedings in the House of Commons with the Speaker.

European parliamentary elections

Elections for the European Parliament are also held every five years. There are 78 seats for representatives from the UK in the European Parliament and elected members are called Members of the European Parliament (MEPs). Elections to the European Parliament use a system of proportional representation, whereby seats are allocated to each party in proportion to the total votes it won.

The House of Lords

Members of the House of Lords, known as peers, are not elected and do not represent a constituency. The role and membership of the House of Lords have recently undergone big changes. Until 1958 all peers were either 'hereditary' meaning that their titles were inherited, senior judges, or bishops of the Church of England. Since 1958 the Prime Minister has had the power to appoint peers just for their own lifetime. These peers, known as Life Peers, have usually had a distinguished career in politics, business, law or some other profession. This means that debates in the House of Lords often draw on more specialist knowledge than is available to members of the House of Commons. Life Peers are appointed by the Queen on the advice of the Prime Minister but they include people nominated by the leaders of the other main parties and by an independent Appointments Commission for non-party peers.

In the last few years the hereditary peers have lost the automatic right to attend the House of Lords, although they are allowed to elect a few of their number to represent them.

While the House of Lords is usually the less important of the two chambers of Parliament, it is more independent of the government. It can suggest amendments or propose new laws, which are then discussed by the House of Commons. The House of Lords can become very important if the majority of its members will not agree to pass a law for which the House of Commons has voted. The House of Commons has powers to overrule the House of Lords, but these are very rarely used.

The Prime Minister

The Prime Minister (PM) is the leader of the political party in power. He or she appoints the members of the Cabinet and has control over many important public appointments. The official home of the Prime Minister is 10 Downing Street, in central

London, near the Houses of Parliament; he or she also has a country house not far from London called Chequers. The Prime Minister can be changed if the MPs in the governing party decide to do so, or if he or she wishes to resign. More usually, the Prime Minister resigns when his or her party is defeated in a general election.

The Cabinet

The Prime Minister appoints about 20 senior MPs to become ministers in charge of departments. These include the Chancellor of the Exchequer, responsible for the economy, the Home Secretary, responsible for law, order and immigration, the Foreign Secretary, and ministers (called 'Secretaries of State') for education, health and defence. The Lord Chancellor, who is the minister responsible for legal affairs, is also a member of the Cabinet but sat in the House of Lords rather than the House of Commons. Following legislation passed in 2005, it is now possible for the Lord Chancellor to sit in the Commons. These ministers form the Cabinet, a small committee which usually meets weekly and makes important decisions about government policy which often then have to be debated or approved by Parliament.

The Opposition

The second largest party in the House of Commons is called the Opposition. The Leader of the Opposition is the person who hopes to become Prime Minister if his or her party wins the next general election. The Leader of the Opposition leads his or her party in pointing out the government's failures and weaknesses; one important opportunity to do this is at Prime Minister Questions which takes place every week while Parliament is sitting. The Leader of the Opposition also appoints senior Opposition MPs to lead the criticism of government ministers, and together they form the Shadow Cabinet.

The Speaker

Debates in the House of Commons are chaired by the Speaker, the chief officer of the House of Commons. The Speaker is politically neutral. He or she is an MP, elected by fellow MPs to keep order during political debates and to make sure the rules are followed. This includes making sure the Opposition has a guaranteed amount of time to debate issues it chooses. The Speaker also represents Parliament at ceremonial occasions.

The party system

Under the British system of parliamentary democracy, anyone can stand for election as an MP but they are unlikely to win an election unless they have been nominated to represent one of the major political parties. These are the Labour Party, the Conservative Party, the Liberal Democrats, or one of the parties representing Scottish, Welsh, or Northern Irish interests. There are just a few MPs who do not represent any of the main political parties and are called 'independents'. The main political parties actively seek members among ordinary voters to join their debates, contribute to their costs, and help at elections for Parliament or for local government; they have branches in most constituencies and they hold policy-making conferences every year.

Pressure and lobby groups

Pressure and lobby groups are organisations that try to influence government policy. They play a very important role in politics. There are many pressure groups in the UK. They may represent economic interests (such as the Confederation of British Industry, the Consumers' Association, or the trade unions) or views on particular subjects (e.g. Greenpeace or Liberty). The general public is more likely to support pressure groups than join a political party.

The civil service

Civil servants are managers and administrators who carry out government policy. They have to be politically neutral and professional, regardless of which political party is in power. Although civil servants have to follow the policies of the elected government, they can warn ministers if they think a policy is impractical or not in the public interest. Before a general election takes place, top civil servants study the Opposition party policies closely in case they need to be ready to serve a new government with different aims and policies.

Devolved administration

In order to give people in Wales and Scotland more control of matters that directly affect them, in 1997 the government began a programme of devolving power from central government. Since 1999 there has been a Welsh Assembly, a Scottish Parliament and, periodically, a Northern Ireland Assembly. Although policy and laws governing defence, foreign affairs, taxation and social security all remain under central UK government control, many other public services now come under the control of the devolved administrations in Wales and Scotland.

Both the Scottish Parliament and Welsh Assembly have been setup using forms of proportional representation which ensures that each party gets a number of seats in proportion to the number of votes they receive. Similarly, proportional representation is used in Northern Ireland in order to ensure 'power sharing' between the Unionist majority (mainly Protestant) and the substantial (mainly Catholic) minority aligned to Irish nationalist parties. A different form of proportional representation is used for elections to the European Parliament.

The Welsh Assembly Government

The National Assembly for Wales, or Welsh Assembly Government (WAG), is situated in Cardiff the capital city of Wales. It has 60 Assembly Members (AMs) and elections are held every four years.

Welsh Assembly in Cardiff

Members can speak in either Welsh or English and all its publications are in both languages. The Assembly has the power to make decisions on important matters such as education policy, the environment, health services, transport and local government, and to pass laws for Wales on these matters within a statutory framework set out by the UK Parliament at Westminster.

The Parliament of Scotland

A long campaign in Scotland for more independence and democratic control led to the formation in 1999 of the Parliament of Scotland, which sits in Edinburgh, the capital city of Scotland.

There are 129 Members of the Scottish Parliament (MSPs), elected by a form of proportional representation. This has led to the sharing of power in Scotland between the Labour and Liberal Democrat parties. The Scottish Parliament can pass legislation for Scotland on all matters that are not specifically reserved to the UK Parliament. The matters on which the Scottish Parliament can legislate include civil and criminal law, health, education, planning and the raising of additional taxes.

The Northern Ireland Assembly

A Northern Ireland Parliament was established in 1922 when Ireland was divided, but it was abolished in 1972 shortly after the Troubles broke out in 1969.

Soon after the end of the Troubles, the Northern Ireland Assembly was established with a power-sharing agreement which distributes ministerial offices among the main parties. The Assembly has 108 elected members known as MLAs (Members of the Legislative Assembly). Decision-making powers devolved to Northern Ireland include education, agriculture, the environment, health and social services in Northern Ireland.

The UK government kept the power to suspend the Northern Ireland Assembly if the political leaders no longer agreed to work together or if the Assembly was not working in the interests of the people of Northern Ireland. This has happened several times and the Assembly is currently suspended (2006). This means that the elected assembly members do not have power to pass bills or make decisions.

Local government

Towns, cities and rural areas in the UK are governed by democratically elected councils, often called local authorities. Some areas have both district and county councils which have different functions, although most larger towns and cities will have a single local authority. Many councils representing towns and cities appoint a mayor who is the ceremonial leader of the council but in some towns a mayor is appointed to be the effective leader of the administration. London has 33 local authorities, with the Greater London Authority and the Mayor of London co-ordinating policies across the capital. Local authorities are required to provide 'mandatory services' in their area. These services include education, housing, social services, passenger transport, the fire service, rubbish collection, planning, environmental health and libraries.

Most of the money for the local authority services comes from the government through taxes. Only about 20% is funded locally through 'council tax' a local tax set by councils to help pay for local services. It applies to all domestic properties, including houses, bungalows, flats, maisonettes, mobile homes or houseboats, whether owned or rented.

Local elections for councillors are held in May every year. Many candidates stand for council election as members of a political party.

The judiciary

In the UK the laws made by Parliament are the highest authority. But often important questions arise about how the laws are to be interpreted in particular cases. It is the task of the judges (who are together called 'the judiciary') to interpret the law, and the government may not interfere with their role. Often the actions of the government are claimed to be illegal and, if the judges agree, then the government must either change its policies or ask Parliament to change the law. This has become all the more important in recent years, as the judges now have the task of applying the Human Rights Act. If they find that a public body is not respecting a person's human rights, they may order that body to change its practices and to pay compensation, if appropriate. If the judges believe that an Act of Parliament is incompatible with the Human Rights Act, they cannot change it themselves but they can ask Parliament to consider doing so.

Judges cannot, however, decide whether people are guilty or innocent of serious crimes. When someone is accused of a serious crime, a jury will decide whether he or she is innocent or guilty and, if guilty, the judge will decide on the penalty. For less important crimes, a magistrate will decide on guilt and on any penalty.

The police

The police service is organised locally, with one police service for each county or group of counties. The largest force is the Metropolitan Police, which serves London and is based at New Scotland Yard. Northern Ireland as a whole is served by the Police Service for Northern Ireland (PSNI). The police have 'operational independence': which means that the

government cannot instruct them on what to do in any particular case. But the powers of the police are limited by the law and their finances are controlled by the government and by police authorities made up of councillors and magistrates. The Independent Police Complaints Commission (or, in Northern Ireland, the Police Ombudsman) investigates serious complaints against the police.

Non-departmental public bodies (quangos)

Non-departmental public bodies, also known as quangos, are independent organisations that carry out functions on behalf of the public which it would be inappropriate to place under the political control of a Cabinet minister. There are many hundreds of these bodies, carrying out a wide variety of public duties. Appointments to these bodies are usually made by ministers, but they must do so in an open and fair way.

The role of the media

Proceedings in Parliament are broadcast on digital television and published in official reports such as Hansard, which is available in large libraries and on the Internet: www.parliament.uk. Most people, however, get information about political issues and events from newspapers (often called the press), television and radio.

The UK has a free press, meaning that what is written in newspapers is free from government control. Newspaper owners and editors hold strong political opinions and run campaigns to try and influence government policy and public opinion. As a result it is sometimes difficult to distinguish fact from opinion in newspaper coverage.

By law, radio and television coverage of the political parties at election periods must be balanced and so equal time has to be given to rival viewpoints. But broadcasters are free to interview politicians in a tough and lively way.

Who can vote?

The United Kingdom has had a fully democratic system since 1928, when women were allowed to vote at 21, the same age as men.

The present voting age of 18 was set in 1969, and (with a few exceptions such as convicted prisoners) all UK-born and naturalised citizens have full civic rights, including the right to vote and do jury service.

Citizens of the UK, the Commonwealth and the Irish Republic (if resident in the UK) can vote in all public elections. Citizens of EU states who are resident in the UK can vote in all elections except national parliamentary (general) elections.

In order to vote in a parliamentary, local or European election, you must have your name on the register of electors, known as the electoral register. If you are eligible to vote, you can register by contacting your local council election registration office. If you don't know what your local authority is, you can find out by telephoning the Local Government Association (LGA) information line on 020 7664 3131 between 9 a.m. and 5 p.m, Monday to Friday. You will have to tell them your postcode or your full address and they will be able to give you the name of your local authority. You can also get voter registration forms in English, Welsh and some other languages on the Internet: www.electoralcommission.org.uk

Contacting elected members

The electoral register is updated every year in September or October. An electoral registration form is sent to every household and it has to be completed and returned, with the names of everyone who is resident in the household and eligible to vote on 15 October.

In Northern Ireland a different system operates. This is called individual registration and all those entitled to vote must complete their own registration form. Once registered, you can stay on the register provided your personal details do not change. For more information telephone the Electoral Office for Northern Ireland on 028 9044 6688.

By law, each local authority has to make its electoral register available for anyone to look at although this now has to be supervised. The register is kept at each local electoral registration office (or council office in England and Wales). It is also possible to see the register at some public buildings such as libraries.

Standing for office

Most citizens of the United Kingdom, the Irish Republic or the Commonwealth aged 18 or over can stand for public office. There are some exceptions and these include members of the armed forces, civil servants and people found guilty of certain criminal offences. Members of the House of Lords may not stand for election to the House of Commons but are eligible for all other public offices.

To become a local councillor, a candidate must have a local connection with the area through work, being on the electoral register, or through renting or owning land or property.

All elected members have a duty to serve and represent their constituents. You can get contact details for all your representatives and their parties from your local library. Assembly members, MSPs, MPs and MEPs are also listed in the phone book and Yellow Pages. You can contact MPs by letter or phone at their constituency office or their office in the House of Commons: The House of Commons, Westminster, London SW1A OAA, or telephone: 020 7729 3000. Many Assembly Members, MSPs, MPs and MEPs hold regular local 'surgeries'. These are often advertised in the local paper and constituents can go and talk about issues in person. You can find out the name of your local MP and get in touch with them by fax through the website: www.writetothem.com. This service is free.

How to visit Parliament and the Devolved Administrations

The public can listen to debates in the Palace of Westminster from public galleries in both the House of Commons and the House of Lords. You can either write to your local MP in advance to ask for tickets or you can queue on the day at the public entrance. Entrance is free. Sometimes there are long queues for the House of Commons and you may have to wait for at least one or two hours. It is usually easier to get into the House of Lords. You can find further information on the UK Parliament website: www.parliament.uk

In Northern Ireland, elected members, known as MLAs, meet in the Northern Ireland Assembly at Stormont, in Belfast. The Northern Ireland Assembly is presently suspended. There are two ways to arrange a visit to Stormont. You can either contact the Education Service (details on the Northern Ireland Assembly website: www.niassembly.gov.uk) or contact an MLA.

In Scotland, the elected members, called MSPs, meet in the Scottish Parliament at Holyrood in Edinburgh (for more information see: www.scottish.parliament.uk).

You can get information, book tickets or arrange tours through the visitor services. You can write to them at The Scottish Parliament, Edinburgh, EH99 1SP, or telephone 0131 348 5200, or email sp.bookings@scottish.parliament.uk

In Wales, the elected members, known as AMs, meet in the Welsh Assembly in the Senedd in Cardiff Bay (for more information see: www.wales.gov.uk). You can book guided tours or seats in the public galleries for the Welsh Assembly. To make a booking, telephone the Assembly booking line on 029 2089 8477 or email:
assembly.booking@wales.gsi.gov.uk

The UK in Europe and the world

The Commonwealth

The Commonwealth is an association of countries, most of which were once part of the British Empire, though a few countries that were not in the Empire have also joined it.

Commonwealth members

Antigua and Barbuda	Mozambique
Australia	Namibia
The Bahamas	Nauru*
Bangladesh	New Zealand
Barbados	Nigeria
Belize	Pakistan
Botswana	Papua New Guinea
Brunei Darussalam	St Kitts and Nevis
Cameroon	St Lucia
Canada	St Vincent and the Grenadines

Cyprus
Dominica
Fiji Islands
The Gambia
Ghana
Grenada
Guyana
India
Jamaica
Kenya
Kiribati
Lesotho
Malawi
Malaysia
Maldives
Malta
Mauritius

Samoa
Seychelles
Sierra Leone
Singapore
Solomon Islands
South Africa
Sri Lanka
Swaziland
Tonga
Trinidad and Tobago
Tuvalu
Uganda
United Kingdom
United Republic of Tanzania
Vanuatu
Zambia
*Nauru is a Special Member

The Queen is the head of the Commonwealth, which currently has 53 member states. Membership is voluntary and the Commonwealth has no power over its members although it can suspend membership. The Commonwealth aims to promote democracy, good government and to eradicate poverty.

The European Union (EU)

The European Union (EU), originally called the European Economic Community (EEC), was set up by six Western European countries who signed the Treaty of Rome on 25 March 1957. One of the main reasons for doing this was the belief that co-operation between states would reduce the likelihood of another war in Europe. Originally the UK decided not to join this group and only became part of the European Union in 1973. In 2004 ten new member countries joined the EU, with a further two in 2006 making a total of 27 member countries.

One of the main aims of the EU today is for member states to function as a single market. Most of the countries of the EU have a shared currency, the euro, but the UK has decided to retain its own currency unless the British people choose to accept the euro in a referendum. Citizens of an EU member state have the right to travel to and work in any EU country if they have a valid passport or identity card. This right can be restricted on the grounds of public health, public order and public security. The right to work is also sometimes restricted for citizens of countries that have joined the EU recently.

The Council of the European Union (usually called the Council of Ministers) is effectively the governing body of the EU. It is made up of government ministers from each country in the EU and, together with the European Parliament is the legislative body of the EU. The Council of Ministers passes EU law on the recommendations of the European Commission and the European Parliament and takes the most important decisions about how the EU is run. The European Commission is based in Brussels, the capital city of Belgium. It is the civil service of the EU and drafts proposals for new EU policies and laws and administers its funding programmes.

The European Parliament meets in Strasbourg, in north-eastern France, and in Brussels. Each country elects members, called Members of the European Parliament (MEPs), every five years. The European Parliament examines decisions made by the European Council and the European Commission, and it has the power to refuse agreement to European laws proposed by the commission and to check on the spending of EU funds.

European Union law is legally binding in the UK and all the other member states. European laws, called directives, regulations or framework decisions, have made a lot of difference to people's rights in the UK, particularly at work. For example, there are EU directives about the procedures for making workers redundant and regulations that limit the number of hours people can be made to work.

The Council of Europe

The Council of Europe was created in 1949 and the UK was one of the founder members. Most of the countries of Europe are members. It has no power to make laws but draws up conventions and charters which focus on human rights, democracy, education, the environment, health and culture. The most important of these is the European Convention on Human Rights; all member states are bound by this Convention and a member state which persistently refuses to obey the Convention may be expelled from the Council of Europe.

The United Nations (UN)

The UK is a member of the United Nations (UN), an international organisation to which over 190 countries now belong. The UN was set up after the Second World War and aims to prevent war and promote international peace and security. There are 15 members on the UN Security Council, which recommends action by the UN when there are international crises and threats to peace. The UK is one of the five permanent members.

Three very important agreements produced by the UN are the Universal Declaration of Human Rights, the Convention on the Elimination of All Forms of Discrimination against Women, and the UN Convention on the Rights of the Child. Although none of these has the force of Law, they are widely used in political debate and legal cases to reinforce the law and to assess the behaviour of countries.

Notes

Chapter 4 – QuickStudy

The monarchy

- Queen Elizabeth II is the Head of State of the United Kingdom and many countries in the Commonwealth.
- The queen or king can advise, warn and encourage the Prime Minister.
- The monarch has important ceremonial roles such as the opening of the new parliamentary session each year.

Parliament

- Parliament is made up of 2 houses, The House of Commons and the House of Lords.
- The House of Commons is the more important of the two chambers in Parliament and its members are democratically elected.
- The system of government in the United Kingdom is a parliamentary democracy. Voters elect 646 Members of Parliament (MPs) for the House of Commons at least every five years. Most MPs belong to a political party and the party with the largest number of MPs forms the government.
- MPs are elected through a system called 'first past the post'. In each constituency, the candidate who gets the most votes is elected.

The Prime Minister and the Cabinet

- The leader of the winning party is called the Prime Minister (PM) who's official residence is 10 Downing Street.
- About 20 senior MPs form the Cabinet, a small committee which usually meets weekly and makes important decisions about government policy. The Cabinet is made up of the Chancellor of the Exchequer, responsible for the economy, the Home Secretary, responsible for law, order and immigration, the Foreign Secretary, and ministers (called 'Secretaries of State') for education, health and defence.
- The Lord Chancellor is also a member of the Cabinet.

The Constitution

- The UK does not have a written constitution.

The Opposition

- The second largest party in the House of Commons is called the Opposition.
- The Leader of the Opposition leads his or her party in pointing out the government's failures and weaknesses.

Proportional representation

- Elections to the European Parliament, Scottish Parliament, Welsh Assembly and Northern Ireland Assembly use a system of proportional representation, whereby seats are allocated to each party in proportion to the total votes it won.

Citizenship

- British citizens, including naturalised citizens, aged 18 years of age and over have the right to vote, stand for Parliament and do jury service.

The judiciary, police and local authorities

- Judges (who are together called 'the judiciary') interpret the law, and the government may not interfere with their role.
- The police service is organised locally, with one police service for each county or group of counties.
- The police have 'operational independence': which means that the government cannot instruct them on what to do in any particular case.
- Towns, cities and rural areas in the UK are governed by democratically elected councils, often called local authorities.
- Local authorities are required to provide 'mandatory services' in their area. These services include education, housing, social services, passenger transport the fire service, rubbish collection, planning, environmental

health and libraries.

Non-departmental public bodies

- Non-departmental public bodies, also known as quangos, are independent organisations that carry out functions on behalf of the public which it would be inappropriate to place under the political control of a Cabinet minister.

The Council of Europe, the European Union, the European Commission and the European Parliament.

- The UK is a member of the Council of Europe
- The Council of the Europe is the governing body of the EU. It is made up of government ministers from each country in the EU.
- The European Union (EU) is made up of 27 member countries. It's main aim EU today is for member states to function as a single market and most of the countries of the EU (not including Britain) have a shared currency, the euro. The UK is a member of the European Union
- The European Commission is the civil service of the EU and drafts proposals for new EU policies and laws and administers its funding programmes.
- European Parliament examines decisions made by the European Council and the European Commission. It has the power to refuse agreement to European laws proposed by the commission, to check on the spending of EU funds and takes the most important decisions about how the EU is run.
- Citizens of an EU member state have the right to travel to and work in any EU country if they have a valid passport or identity card. This right can be restricted on the grounds of public health, public order and public security. The right to work is also sometimes restricted for citizens of countries that have joined the EU recently.

The UN and the Commonwealth

- The UN was set up after the Second World War and aims to prevent war and promote international peace and security. The UK is a member of the United Nations and one of the five permanent members of the UN Security Council.
- The UK is also a member of the Commonwealth, an association of countries, most of which were once part of the British Empire. The Commonwealth aims to promote democracy, good government and to eradicate poverty.

Chapter 5 – EVERYDAY NEEDS

Housing

Buying a home

Two-thirds of people in the UK own their own home. Most other people rent houses, flats or rooms.

Mortgages

People who buy their own home usually pay for it with a mortgage, a special loan from a bank or building society. This loan is paid back, with interest over a long period of time, usually 25 years. You can get information about mortgages from a bank or building society. Some banks can also give information about Islamic (Sharia) mortgages.

If you are having problems paying your mortgage repayments, you can get help and advice. It is important to speak to your bank or building society as soon as you can.

Estate agents

If you wish to buy a home, usually the first place to start is an estate agent. In Scotland the process is different and you should go first to a solicitor. Estate

agents represent the person selling their house or flat. They arrange for buyers to visit homes that are for sale. There are estate agents in all towns and cities and they usually have websites where they advertise the homes for sale. You can also find details about homes for sale on the internet and in national and local newspapers.

Making an offer

In the UK, except in Scotland, when you find a home you wish to buy you have to make an offer to the seller. You usually do this through an estate agent or solicitor. Many people offer a lower price than the seller is asking. Your first offer must be 'subject to contract' so that you can withdraw if there are reasons why you cannot complete the purchase. In Scotland the seller sets a price and buyers make offers over that amount. The agreement becomes legally binding earlier than it does elsewhere in the UK.

Solicitor and surveyor

It is important that a solicitor helps you through the process of buying a house or flat. When you make an offer on a property, the solicitor will carry out a number of legal checks on the property, the seller and the local area. The solicitor will provide the legal agreements necessary for you to buy the property. The bank or building society that is providing you with your mortgage will also

carry out checks on the house or flat you wish to buy. These are done by a surveyor. The buyer does not usually see the result of this survey, so the buyer often asks a second surveyor to check the house as well. In Scotland the survey is carried out before an offer is made, to help people decide how much they want to bid for the property.

Rented accommodation

It is possible to rent accommodation from the local authority (the council), from a housing association or from private property owners called landlords.

The local authority

Most local authorities (or councils) provide housing. This is often called council housing: In Northern Ireland social housing is provided by the Northern Ireland Housing Executive (www.nihe.co.uk). In Scotland you can find information on social housing at: www.sfha.co.uk. Everyone is entitled to apply for council accommodation. To apply you must put your name on the council register or list. This is available from the housing department at the local authority. You are then assessed according to your needs. This is done through a system of points. You get more points if you have priority needs, for example if you are homeless and have children or chronic ill health.

It is important to note that in many areas of the UK there is a shortage of council accommodation, and that some people have to wait a very long time for a house or flat.

Housing associations

Housing associations are independent not-for-profit organisations which provide housing for rent. In some areas they have taken over the administration of local authority housing. They also run schemes called shared ownership, which help people buy part of a house or flat if they cannot afford to buy all of it at once. There are usually waiting lists for homes owned by housing associations.

Privately rented accommodation

Many people rent houses or flats privately, from landlords. Information about private accommodation can be found in local newspapers, notice boards, estate agents and letting agents.

Tenancy agreement

When you rent a house or flat privately you sign a tenancy agreement, or lease. This explains the conditions or 'rules' you must follow while renting the property. This agreement must be checked very carefully to avoid problems later. The agreement also contains a list of any furniture or fittings in the property. This is called an inventory. Before you sign the agreement check the details and keep it safe during your tenancy.

Deposit and rent

You will probably be asked to give the landlord a deposit at the beginning of your tenancy. This is to cover the cost of any damage. It is usually equal to one month's rent. The landlord must return this money to you at the end of your tenancy, unless you have caused damage to the property.

Your rent is fixed with your landlord at the beginning of the tenancy. The landlord cannot raise the rent without your agreement.

If you have a low income or are unemployed you may be able to claim Housing Benefit to help you pay your rent.

Renewing and ending a tenancy

Your tenancy agreement will be for a fixed period of time, often six months. After this time the tenancy can be ended or, if both tenant and landlord agree, renewed. If you end the tenancy before the fixed time, you usually have to pay the rent for the agreed full period of the tenancy.

A landlord cannot force a tenant to leave. If a landlord wishes a tenant to leave they must follow the correct procedures. These vary according to the type of tenancy. It is a criminal offence for a landlord to use threats or violence against a tenant or to force them to leave without an order from court.

Discrimination

It is unlawful for a landlord to discriminate against someone looking for accommodation because of their sex, race, nationality, or ethnic group, or because they are disabled, unless the landlord or a close relative of the landlord is sharing the accommodation.

Homelessness

If you are homeless you should go for help to the local authority (or, in Northern Ireland, the Housing Executive). They have a legal duty to offer help and advice, but will not offer you a place to live unless you have priority need and have a connection with the area, such as work or family. You must also show that you have not made yourself intentionally homeless.

Help

If you are homeless or have problems with your landlord, help can be found from the following:

- The housing department of the local authority will give advice on homelessness and on Housing Benefit as well as deal with problems you may have in council-owned property

- The Citizens Advice Bureau will give advice on all types of housing problems. There may also be a housing advice centre in your neighbourhood.

- Shelter is a housing charity which runs a 24-hour helpline on 0808 800 4444, or visit www.shelternet.org.uk

- Help with the cost of moving and setting up home may be available from the Social Fund. This is run by the Department for Work and Pensions (DWP). It provides grants and loans such as the Community Care Grant for people setting up home after being homeless or after they have been in prison or other institutions. Other loans are available for people who have had an emergency such as flooding. Information about these is available at the Citizens Advice Bureau or Jobcentre Plus.

Services in and for the home

Water

Water is supplied to all homes in the UK. The charge for this is called the water rates. When you move in to a new home (bought or rented), you should receive a letter telling you the name of the company responsible for supplying your water. The water rates may be paid in one payment (a lump sum) or in instalments, usually monthly. If you receive Housing Benefit, you should check to see if this covers the water rates. The cost of the water usually depends on the size of your property, but some homes have a water meter which tells you exactly how much water you have used. In Northern Ireland water is currently (2006) included in the domestic rates, although this may change in future.

Electricity and gas

All properties in the UK have electricity supplied at 240 volts. Most homes also have gas. When you move into a new home or leave an old one, you should make a note of the electricity and gas meter readings. If you have an urgent problem with your gas, electricity or water supply, you can ring a 24-hour helpline. This can be found on your bill, in the Yellow Pages or in the phone book.

Gas and electricity suppliers

It is possible to choose between different gas and electricity suppliers. These have different prices and different terms and conditions. Get advice before you sign a contract with a new supplier. To find out which company supplies your gas, telephone Transco on 0870 608 1524.

To find out which company supplies your electricity, telephone Energywatch on 0845 906 0708 or visit www.energywatch.org.uk. Energywatch can also give you advice on changing your supplier of electricity or gas.

Telephone

Most homes already have a telephone line (called a land line). If you need a new line, telephone BT on 150442, or contact a cable company. Many companies offer land line, mobile telephone and broadband internet services. You can get advice about prices or about changing your company from Ofcom at www.ofcom.org.uk. You can call from public payphones using cash, pre-paid phonecards or credit or debit cards. Calls made from hotels and hostels are usually more expensive. Dial 999 or 112 for emergency calls for police, fire or ambulance service. These calls are free. Do not use these numbers if it is not a real emergency; you can always find the local numbers for these services in the phone book.

Bills

Information on how to pay for water, gas, electricity and the telephone is found on the back of each bill. If you have a bank account you can pay your bills by standing order or direct debit. Most companies operate a budget scheme which allows you to pay a fixed sum every month. If you do not pay a bill, the service can be cut off. To get a service reconnected, you have to pay another charge.

Refuse collection

Refuse is also called waste, or rubbish. The local authority collects the waste regularly, usually on the same day of each week. Waste must be put outside in a particular place to get collected. In some parts of the country the waste is put into plastic bags, in others it is put into bins with wheels. In many places you must recycle your rubbish, separating paper, glass, metal or plastic from the other rubbish. Large objects which you want to throw away, such as a bed, a wardrobe or a fridge, need to be collected separately. Contact the local authority to arrange this. If you have a business, such as a factory or a shop, you must make special arrangements with the local authority for your waste to be collected. It is a criminal offence to dump rubbish anywhere.

Council Tax

Local government services, such as education, police, roads, refuse collection and libraries, are paid for partly by grants from the government and partly by Council Tax (see chapter 4 – Local Government). In Northern Ireland there is a system of domestic rates instead of the Council Tax. The amount of Council Tax you pay depends on the size and value of your house or flat (dwelling). You must register to pay Council Tax when you move into a new property, either as the owner or the tenant. You can pay the tax in one payment, in two instalments, or in ten instalments (from April to January).

If only one person lives in the flat or house, you get a 25% reduction on your Council Tax. (This does not apply in Northern Ireland). You may also get a reduction if someone in the property has a disability. People on a low income or who receive benefits such as Income Support or Jobseeker's Allowance can get Council Tax Benefit. You can get advice on this from the local authority or the Citizens Advice Bureau.

Buildings and household insurance

If you buy a home with a mortgage, you must insure the building against fire, theft and accidental damage. The landlord should arrange insurance for rented buildings. It is also wise to insure your possessions against theft or damage. There are many companies that provide insurance.

Neighbours

If you live in rented accommodation, you will have a tenancy agreement. This explains all the conditions of your tenancy. It will probably include information on what to do if you have problems with your housing. Occasionally, there may be problems with your neighbours. If you do have problems with your neighbours, they can usually be solved by speaking to them first. If you cannot solve the problem, speak to your landlord, local authority or housing association.

Keep a record of the problems in case you have to show exactly what the problems are and when they started. Neighbours who cause a very serious nuisance may be taken to court and can be evicted from their home.

There are several mediation organisations which help neighbours to solve their disputes without having to go to court. Mediators talk to both sides and try to find a solution acceptable to both. You can get details of mediation organisations from the local authority, Citizens Advice, and Mediation UK on 01179046661 or visit: www.mediationuk.co.uk.

Money and credit

Bank notes in the UK come in denominations (values) of £5, £10, £20 and £50. Northern Ireland and Scotland have their own bank notes which are valid everywhere in the UK, though sometimes people may not realise this and may not wish to accept them.

The euro

In January 2002 twelve European Union (EU) states adopted the euro as their common currency. The UK government decided not to adopt the euro at that time, and has said it will only do so if the British people vote for the euro in a referendum. The euro does circulate to some extent in Northern Ireland, particularly in the towns near the border with Ireland.

Foreign currency

You can get or change foreign currency at banks, building societies, large post offices and exchange shops or bureaux de change. You might have to order some currencies in advance. The exchange rates vary and you should check for the best deal.

Banks and building societies

Most adults in the UK have a bank or building society account. Many large national banks or building societies have branches in towns and cities throughout the UK. It is worth checking the different types of account each one offers. Many employers pay salaries directly into a bank or building society account. There are many banks and building societies to choose from. To open an account you need to show documents to prove your identity, such as a passport, immigration document or driving licence. You also need to show something with your address on it like a tenancy agreement or household bill. It is also possible to open bank accounts in some supermarkets or on the internet.

Cash and debit cards

Cash cards allow you to use cash machines to withdraw money from your account. For this you need a Personal Identification Number (PIN) which you must keep secret. A debit card allows you to pay for things without using cash. You must have enough money in your account to cover what you buy. If you lose your cash card or debit card you must inform the bank immediately.

Credit and store cards

Credit cards can be used to buy things in shops, on the telephone and over the internet. A store card is like a credit card but used only in a specific shop. Credit and store cards do not draw money from your bank account but you will be sent a bill every month. If you do not pay the total amount on the bill, you are charged interest. Although credit and store cards are useful, the interest is usually very high and many people fall into debt this way. If you lose your credit or store cards you must inform the company immediately.

Credit and loans

People in the UK often borrow money from banks and other organisations to pay for things like household goods, cars and holidays. This is more common in the UK than in many other countries. You must be very sure of the terms and conditions when you decide to take out a loan. You can get advice on loans from the Citizens Advice Bureau if you are uncertain.

Being refused credit

Banks and other organisations use different information about you to make a decision about a loan, such as your occupation, address, salary and previous credit record. If you apply for a loan you might be refused. If this happens, you have the right to ask the reason why.

Credit unions

Credit unions are financial co-operatives owned and controlled by their members. The members pool their savings and then make loans from this pool. Interest rates in credit unions are usually lower than banks and building societies. There are credit unions in many cities and towns. To find the nearest credit union contact the Association of British Credit Unions (ABCUL) on: www.abcul.coop

Insurance

As well as insuring their property and possessions, many people insure their credit cards and mobile phones. They also buy insurance when they travel abroad in case they lose their luggage or need medical treatment. Insurance is compulsory if you have a car or motorcycle. You can usually arrange insurance directly with an insurance company, or you can use a broker who will help you get the best deal.

Social security

The UK has a system of social security which pays welfare benefits to people who do not have enough money to live on. Benefits are usually available for the sick and disabled, older people, the unemployed and those on low incomes. People who do not have legal rights of residence (or 'settlement') in the UK cannot usually receive benefits.

Arrangements for paying and receiving benefits are complex because they have to cover people in many different situations. Guides to benefits are available from Jobcentre Plus offices, local libraries, post offices and the Citizens Advice Bureau.

Health

Healthcare in the UK is organised under the National Health Service (NHS). The NHS began in 1948, and is one of the largest organisations in Europe. It provides all residents with free healthcare and treatment.

Finding a doctor

Family doctors are called General Practitioners (GPs) and they work in surgeries. GPs often work together in a group practice. This is sometimes called a Primary Health Care Centre.

Your GP is responsible for organising the health treatment you receive. Treatment can be for physical and mental illnesses. If you need to see a specialist, you must go to your GP first. Your GP will then refer you to a specialist in a hospital. Your GP can also refer you for specialist treatment if you have special needs.

You can get a list of local GPs from libraries, post offices, the tourist information office, the Citizens Advice Bureau, the local Health Authority and from the following websites:

www.nhs.uk/ for health practitioners in England;
www.wales.nhs.uk/directory.cfm for health practitioners in Wales;
www.n-i.nhs.uk for health practitioners in Northern Ireland;
www.show.scot.nhs.uk/findnearest/healthservices in Scotland. You can also ask
neighbours and friends for the name of their local doctor.

You can attend a hospital without a GP's letter only in the case of an
emergency. If you have an emergency you should go to the Accident and
Emergency (A & E) department of the nearest hospital.

Registering with a GP

You should look for a GP as soon as you move to a new area. You should not
wait until you are ill. The health centre, or surgery, will tell you what you need to
do to register. Usually you must have a medical card. If you do not have one,
the GP's receptionist should give you a form to send to the local health
authority. They will then send you a medical card. Before you register you
should check the surgery can offer what you need. For example, you might
need a woman GP or maternity services. Sometimes GPs have many patients
and are unable to accept new ones. If you cannot find a GP, you can ask your
local health authority to help you find one.

Using your doctor

All patients registering with a GP are entitled to a free health check.
Appointments to see the GP can be made by phone or in person. Sometimes
you might have to wait several days before you can see a doctor. If you need
immediate medical attention ask for an urgent appointment. You should go to
the GP's surgery a few minutes before the appointment. If you cannot attend or
do not need the appointment any more, you must let the surgery know. The GP
needs patients to answer all questions as fully as possible in order to find out
what is wrong. Everything you tell the GP is completely confidential and cannot
be passed on to anyone else without your permission. If you do not understand
something, ask for clarification. If you have difficulties with English, bring
someone who can help you, or ask the receptionist for an interpreter. This must
be done when you make the appointment. If you have asked for an interpreter,

it is important that you keep your appointment because this service is expensive.

In exceptional circumstances, GPs can visit patients at home but they always give priority to people who are unable to travel. If you call the GP outside normal working hours, you will have to answer several questions about your situation. This is to assess how serious your case is. You will then be told if a doctor can come to your home. You might be advised to go to the nearest A & E department

Charges

Treatment from the GP is free but you have to pay a charge for your medicines and for certain services, such as vaccinations for travel abroad. If the GP decides you need to take medicine you will be given a prescription. You must take this to a pharmacy (chemist).

Prescriptions

- Prescriptions are free for anyone who is

- under 16 years of age (under 25 in Wales)

- under 19 and in full-time education

- aged 60 or over

- pregnant or with a baby under 12 months old

- suffering from a specified medical condition

- receiving Income Support, Jobseekers' Allowance, Working Families or Disabilities Tax Credit

Feeling unwell

If you or your child feels unwell you have the following options:

For information or advice

- ask your local pharmacist (chemist). The pharmacy can give advice on medicines and some illnesses and conditions that are not serious

- speak to a nurse by phoning NHS Direct on 0845 4647

- use the NHS Direct website, NHS Direct Online: www.nhsdirect.nhs.uk

To see a doctor or nurse

- make an appointment to see your GP or a nurse working in the surgery

- visit an NHS walk-in centre.

For urgent medical treatment

- contact your GP

- go to your nearest hospital with an Accident and Emergency department

- call 999 for an ambulance. Calls are free. ONLY use this service for a real emergency.

NHS Direct is a 24-hour telephone service which provides information on particular health conditions. Telephone: 0845 4647. You may ask for an interpreter for advice in your own language. In Scotland, NHS24 at: www.nhs24.com telephone 0845 424 2424.

NHS Direct Online is a website providing information about health services and several medical conditions and treatments: www.nhsdirect.nhs.uk

NHS walk-in centres provide treatment for minor injuries and illnesses seven days a week. You do

not need an appointment. For details of your nearest centre call NHS Direct or visit the NHS website at: www.nhs.uk (for Northern Ireland www.n-i.nhs.uk) and click on 'local NHS services'.

Going into hospital

If you need minor tests at a hospital, you will probably attend the Outpatients department. If your treatment takes several hours, you will go into hospital as a day patient. If you need to stay overnight, you will go into hospital as an in-patient.

You should take personal belongings with you, such as a towel, night clothes, things for washing, and a dressing gown. You will receive all your meals while you are an in-patient. If you need advice about going into hospital, contact Customer Services or the Patient Advice and Liaison Service (PALS) at the hospital where you will receive treatment.

Dentists

You can get the name of a dentist by asking at the local library, at the Citizens Advice Bureau and through NHS Direct. Most people have to pay for dental treatment. Some dentists work for the NI-IS and some are private. NHS dentists charge less than private dentists, but some dentists have two sets of charges, both NHS and private. A dentist should explain your treatment and the charges before the treatment begins.

Free dental treatment is available to

- people under 18 (in Wales people under 25 and over 60) pregnant women and women with babies under 12 months old

- people on income support, Jobseekers' Allowance or Pension Credit Guarantee

Opticians

Most people have to pay for sight tests and glasses, except children, people over 60, people with certain eye conditions and people receiving certain benefits. In Scotland, eye tests are free.

Pregnancy and care of young children

If you are pregnant you will receive regular ante-natal care. This is available from your local hospital, local health centre or from special antenatal clinics. You will receive support from a GP and from a midwife. Midwives work in hospitals or health centres. Some GPs do not provide maternity services so you may wish to look for another GP during your pregnancy. In the UK women usually have their babies in hospital, especially if it is their first baby. It is common for the father to attend the birth, but only if the mother wants him to be there.

A short time after you have your child, you will begin regular contact with a health visitor. She or he is a qualified nurse and can advise you about caring for your baby. The first visits will be in your home, but after that you might meet the health visitor at a clinic. You can ask advice from your health visitor until your child is five years old. In most towns and cities there are mother and toddler groups or playgroups for small children. These often take place at local churches and community centres. You might be able to send your child to a nursery school.

Information on pregnancy

You can get information on maternity and ante-natal services in your area from your local health authority, a health visitor or your GP. The number of your health authority will be in the phone book.

The Family Planning Association (FPA) gives advice on contraception and sexual health. The FPA helpline is 0845 310 1334, or: www.fpa.org.uk. The National Childbirth Trust gives information and support in pregnancy, childbirth and early parenthood: www.nctpregnancyandbabycare.com

Registering a birth

Your must register your baby with the Registrar of Births, Marriages and Deaths (Register Office) within six weeks of the birth. The address of your local Register Office is in the phone book. If the parents are married, either the mother or father can register the birth. If they are not married, only the mother can register the birth. If the parents are not married but want both names on the child's birth certificate, both mother and father must be present when they register their baby.

Education

Going to school

Education in the UK is free and compulsory for all children between the ages of 5 and 16 (4 to 16 in Northern Ireland). The education system varies in England, Scotland, Wales and Northern Ireland.

The child, parent or guardian is responsible for making sure their child goes to school, arrives on time and attends for the whole school year. If they do not do this, the parent or guardian may be prosecuted.

Some areas of the country offer free nursery education for children over the age of 3. In most parts of the UK, compulsory education is divided into two stages, primary and secondary. In some places there is a middle-school system. In England and Wales the primary stage lasts from 5 to 11, in Scotland from 5 to 12 and in Northern Ireland from 4 to 11. The secondary stage lasts until the age of 16. At that age young people can choose to leave school or to continue with their education until they are 17 or 18.

Details of local schools are available from your local education authority office or website. The addresses and phone numbers of local education authorities are in the phone book.

Primary schools

These are usually schools where both boys and girls learn together and are usually close to a child's home. Children tend to be with the same group and teacher all day. Schools encourage parents to help their children with learning, particularly with reading and writing.

Secondary schools

At age 11(12 in Scotland) children go to secondary school. This might normally be the school nearest their home, but parents in England and Wales are allowed to express a preference for a different school. In some areas, getting a secondary school place in a preferred school can be difficult, and parents often apply to several schools in order to make sure their child gets offered a place. In Northern Ireland many schools select children through a test taken at the age of 11.

If the preferred school has enough places, the child will be offered a place. If there are not enough places, children will be offered places according to the school's admission arrangements. Admission arrangements vary from area to area.

Secondary schools are larger than primary schools. Most are mixed sex, although there are single sex schools in some areas. Your local education authority will give you information on schools in your area. It will also tell you which schools have spaces and give you information about why some children will be given places when only a few are available and why other children might not. It will also tell you how to apply for a secondary school place.

Costs

Education at state schools in the UK is free, but parents have to pay for school uniforms and sportswear. There are sometimes extra charges for music lessons and for school outings. Parents on low incomes can get help with costs, and with the cost of school meals. You can get advice on this from the local education authority or the Citizens Advice Bureau.

Church and other faith schools

Some primary and secondary schools in the UK are linked to the Church of England or the Roman Catholic Church. These are called 'faith schools'. In some areas there are Muslim, Jewish and Sikh schools. In Northern Ireland, some schools are called Integrated Schools. These schools aim to bring children of different religions together. Information on faith schools is available from your local education authority.

Independent schools

Independent schools are private schools. They are not run or paid for by the state. Independent secondary schools are also sometimes called public schools. There are about 2,500 independent schools in the UK. About 8% of children go to these schools. At independent schools

parents must pay the full cost of their child's education. Some independent schools offer scholarships which pay some or all of the costs of the child's education.

The school curriculum

All state, primary and secondary schools in England, Wales and Northern Ireland follow the National Curriculum. This covers English, maths, science, design and technology, information and communication technology (ICT), history, geography, modern foreign languages, art and design, music, physical education (PE) and citizenship. In Wales, children learn Welsh.

In some primary schools in Wales, all the lessons are taught in Welsh. In Scotland, pupils follow a broad curriculum informed by national guidance. Schools must, by law, provide religious education (RE) to all pupils. Parents are allowed to withdraw their children from these lessons. RE lessons have a Christian basis but children also learn about the other major religions.

Assessment

In England, the curriculum is divided into four stages, called Key Stages. After each stage children are tested. They take Key Stage tests (also called SATs) at ages 7, 11 and 14. At 16 they usually take the General Certificates of Secondary Education (GCSEs) in several subjects, although some schools also offer other qualifications. At 18, young people who have stayed at school do AGCEs (Advanced GCE levels) often just called A levels.

In Wales, schools follow the Welsh National Curriculum but have abolished national tests for children at age 7 and 11. There are also plans in Wales to stop testing children at 14. Teachers in Wales still have to assess and report on their pupils' progress and achievements at 7 and 11.

In Scotland, the curriculum is divided into two phases. The first phase is from 5 to 14. There are six levels in this phase, levels A to F. There are no tests for whole groups during this time. Teachers test individual children when they are ready. From 14 to 16, young people do Standard Grade. After 16 they can study at Intermediate, Higher or Advanced level. In Scotland there will soon be a single curriculum for all pupils from age 3 to age 18. This is called A Curriculum for Excellence. More information can be found at www.acurriculumforexcellencescotland.gov.uk.

Help with English

If your child's main language is not English, the school may arrange for extra language support from an EAL (English Additional Language) specialist teacher.

Careers education

All children get careers advice from the age of 14. Advice is also available from Connexions, a national service for young people: telephone 0808 001 3219 or: www.connexions-direct.com in England. In Wales, Careers Wales offers advice to children from the age of 11. For further information visit: www.careerswales.com or telephone 0800 100 900.

In Scotland, Careers Scotland provides information, services and support to all ages and stages. For further information visit www.careers-scotland.org.uk or telephone 0845 850 2502.

Parents and schools

Many parents are involved with their child's school. A number of places on a school governing body are reserved for parents. The governing body decides how the school is run and administered and produces reports on the progress of the school from year to year. In Scotland, parents can be members of school boards or parent councils.

Schools must be open 190 days a year. Term dates are decided by the governing body or by the local education authority. Children must attend the whole school year. Schools expect parents and guardians to inform them if their child is going to be absent from school. All schools ask parents to sign a home-school agreement. This is a list of things that both the school and the parent or guardian agree to do to ensure a good education for the child. All parents receive a report every year on their child's progress. They also have the chance to go to the school to talk to their child's teachers.

Further education and adult education

At 16, young people can leave school or stay on to do A levels (Higher grades in Scotland) in preparation for university. Some young people go to their local further education (FE) college to improve their exam grades or to get new qualifications for a career. Most courses are free up to the age of 19. Young people from families with low incomes can get financial help with their studies when they leave school at 16. This is called the Education Maintenance Allowance (EMA). Information about this is available at your local college or at: www.dfes.gov.uk.

Further education colleges also offer courses to adults over the age of 18. These include courses for people wishing to improve their skills in English. These courses are called ESOL (English for Speakers of Other Languages). There are also courses for English speakers who need to improve their literacy and numeracy and for people who need to learn new skills for employment ESOL courses are also available in community centres and training centres. There is sometimes a waiting list for ESOL courses because demand is high. In England and Wales, ESOL literacy and numeracy courses are also called Skills for Life courses. You can get information at your local college or local library or from learndirect on 0800 100 900.

Many people join other adult education classes to learn a new skill or hobby and to meet new people. Classes are very varied and range from sports to learning a musical instrument or a new language. Details are usually available from your local library, college or adult education centre.

University

More young people go to university now than in the past. Many go after A levels (or Higher grades in Scotland) at age 18 but it is also possible to go to university later in life. At present most students in England, Wales and Northern Ireland have to pay towards the cost of their tuition fees and to pay for their living expenses. In Scotland there are no tuition fees but after students finish university they pay back some of the cost of their education in a payment called an endowment. At present, universities can charge up to £3,000 per year for their tuition fees, but students do not have to pay anything towards their fees before or during their studies. The government pays their tuition fees and then charges for them when a student starts working after university. Some families on low incomes receive help with their children tuition fees. This is called a grant. The universities also give help, in the form of bursaries. Most students get a low-interest student loan from a bank. This pays for their living costs while they are at university. When a student finishes university and starts working, he or she must pay back the loan.

Leisure

Information

Information about theatre, cinema, music and exhibitions is found in local newspapers, local libraries and tourist information offices. Many museums and art galleries are free.

Film, video and DVD

Films in the UK have a system to show if they are suitable for children. This is called the classification system. If a child is below the age of the classification, they should not watch the film at a cinema or on DVD. All films receive a classification, as follows:

U (Universal): suitable for anyone aged 4 years and over
PG (parental guidance): suitable for everyone but some parts of the film might be unsuitable for children. Their parents should decide.
12 or 12a: children under 12 are not allowed to see or rent the film unless they are with an adult
15: children under 15 are not allowed to see or rent the film.
18: no one under 18 is allowed to see or rent the film.
R18: no one under 18 is allowed to see the film, which is only available in specially licensed cinemas.

Television and radio

Anyone in the UK with a television (TV), DVD or video recorder, computer or any device which is used for watching or recording TV programmes must be covered by a valid television licence. One licence covers all of the equipment at one address, but people who rent different rooms in a shared house must each buy a separate licence.

A colour TV licence currently costs £131.50 (2006) and lasts for 12 months. People aged 75, or over can apply for a free TV licence. Blind people can claim a 50% discount on their TV licence. You risk prosecution and a fine if you watch TV but are not covered by a TV licence. There are many ways to buy a TV licence including from local

Pay Point outlets or on-line at: www.tvlicensing.co.uk. It is also possible to pay

for the licence in instalments. For more information telephone 0870 576 3763 or write to TV Licensing, Bristol BS98 1TL

Sports, clubs and societies

Information about local clubs and societies can usually be found at local libraries or through your local authority. For information about sports you should ask in the local leisure centre, libraries and leisure centres often organise activities for children during the school holidays.

Places of interest

The UK has a large network of public footpaths in the countryside. Many parts of the countryside and places of interest are kept open by the National Trust. This is a charity that works to preserve important buildings and countryside in the UK. Information about National Trust buildings and areas open to the public is available on: www.nationaltrust.org.uk

Pubs and night clubs

Public houses, or pubs, are an important part of social life in the UK. To drink alcohol in a pub you must be 18 or over. People under 18 are not allowed to

buy alcohol in a supermarket or in an off-licence either. The landlord of the pub may allow people of 14 to come into the pub but they are not allowed to drink. At 16, people can drink wine or beer with a meal in a hotel or restaurant.

Pubs are usually open during the day and until 11p.m. If a pub wants to stay open later, it must apply for a special licence. Night clubs open and close later than pubs.

Betting and gambling

People under 18 are not allowed into betting shops or gambling clubs. There is a National Lottery for which draws, with large prizes, are made every week. You can enter by buying a ticket or a scratch card. People under 16 are not allowed to buy a lottery ticket or scratch card.

Pets

Many people in the UK have pets such as cats and dogs. It is against the law to treat a pet cruelly or to neglect it. All dogs in public places must wear a collar showing the name and address of the owner. The owner is responsible for keeping the dog under control and for cleaning up after the animal in a public place. Vaccinations and medical treatment for animals are available from veterinary surgeons (vets). If you cannot afford to pay a vet, you can go to a charity called the PDSA (People's Dispensary for Sick Animals).

To find your nearest branch, visit: www.pdsa.org.uk

Travel and transport

Trains, buses and coaches

For information about trains telephone the National Rail Enquiry Service: 0845 748 4950 or visit: www.nationalrail.co.uk For trains in Northern Ireland, phone Translink on 028 90 66 66 30 or visit: www.translink.co.uk For information about local bus times phone 0870 608 250. For information on coaches, telephone National Express on 08705 80 80 80, or visit: www.nationalexpress.com For coaches in Scotlsand, telephone Scottish Citylink on 08705 50 50 50 or visit www.citylink.co.uk For Northern Ireland, visit: www.translink.co.uk

Usually, tickets for trains and underground systems such as the

London Underground must be bought before you get on the train. The fare varies according to the day and time you wish to travel, Travelling in the rush hour is always more expensive. Discount tickets are available for families, people aged 60 and over, disabled people, students and people under 26. Ask at your local train station for details. Failure to buy a ticket may result in a penalty.

Taxis

To operate legally, all taxis and minicabs must be licensed and display a licence plate. Taxis and cabs with no licence are not insured for fare-paying passengers and are not always safe. Women should not use unlicensed minicabs.

Driving

You must be at least 17 to drive a car or motorcycle, 18 to drive a medium sized lorry, and 21 to drive a large lorry or bus. To drive a lorry, minibus or bus with more than eight passenger seats, you must have a special licence.

If your driving licence is from a country in the European Union (EU), Iceland, Liechtenstein or Norway, you can drive in the UK for as long as your licence is valid.

The driving licence

You must have a driving licence to drive on public roads. To get a driving licence you must pass a test. There are many driving schools where you can learn with the help of a qualified instructor.

You get a full driving licence in three stages:

1. Apply for a provisional licence. You need this licence while you are learning to drive. With this you are allowed to drive a motorcycle up to 125cc or a car. You must put L plates on the vehicle, or D plates in Wales. Learner drivers cannot drive on a motorway. If you drive a car, you must be with someone who is over 21 and who has had a full licence for over three years. You can get an application form for a provisional licence from a post office.

2.   Pass a written theory test.

3.   Pass a practical driving test

Drivers may use their licence until they are 70. After that the licence is valid for three years at a time.

In Northern Ireland, a newly-qualified driver must display an R-Plate (for registered driver) for one year after passing the test.

Overseas licences

If you have a licence from a country outside the EU, you may use it in the UK for up to 12 months. During this time you must get a UK provisional driving licence and pass both the UK theory and practical driving tests, or you will not be able to drive after 12 months.

Insurance

It is a criminal offence to have a car without proper motor insurance. Drivers without insurance can receive very high fines. It is also illegal to allow someone to use your car if they are not insured to drive it.

Road tax and MOT

You must also pay a tax to drive your car on the roads. This is called road tax. Your vehicle must have a road tax disc which shows you have paid. You can buy this at the post office. If you do not pay the road tax, your vehicle may be clamped or towed away.

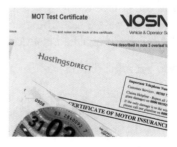

If your vehicle is over three years old, you must take it every year for a Ministry of Transport (MOT) test. You can do this at an approved garage. The garage will give you an MOT certificate when your car passes the test.
It is an offence not to have an MOT certificate. If you do not have an MOT certificate, your insurance will not be valid.

Safety

Everyone in a vehicle should wear a seat belt. Children under 12 years of age may need a special booster seat. Motorcyclists and their passengers must wear a crash helmet (this law does not apply to Sikh men if they are wearing a turban). It is illegal to drive while holding a mobile phone.

Speed limits

For cars and motorcycles the speed limits are:

30 miles per hour (mph) in built-up areas, unless a sign shows a different limit
60 mph on single carriageways
70 mph on motorways and dual carriageways

Speed limits are lower for buses, lorries and cars pulling caravans.

It is illegal to drive when you are over the alcohol limit or drunk. The police can stop you and give you a test to see how much alcohol you have in your body. This is called a breathalyser test. If a driver has more than the permitted amount of alcohol (called being 'over the limit') or refuses to take the test, he or she will be arrested. People who drink and drive can expect to be disqualified from driving for a long period.

Accidents

If you are involved in a road accident

- don't drive away without stopping – this is a criminal offence

- call the police and ambulance on 999 or 112 if someone is injured

- get the names, addresses, vehicle registration numbers and insurance details of the other drivers

- give your details to the other drivers or passengers and to the police

- make a note of everything that happened and contact your insurance company as soon as possible.

Note that if you admit the accident was your fault, the insurance company may refuse to pay. It is better to wait until the insurance company decides for itself whose fault the accident was.

Identity documents

At present, UK citizens do not have to carry identity (ID) cards. The government is, however, making plans to introduce them in the next few years.

Proving your identity

You may have to prove your identity at different times, such as when you open a bank account rent accommodation, enrol for a college course, hire a car, apply for benefits such as housing benefit or apply for a marriage certificate. Different organisations may ask for different documents as proof of identity. These can include:

- official documents from the Home Office showing your immigration status

- a certificate of identity

- a passport or travel document

- a National Insurance (NI) number card

- a provisional or full driving licence

- a recent gas, electricity or phone bill showing your name and address

- a rent or benefits book.

Chapter 5 — QuickStudy

Buying a property

- Usually the first place to start when buying a home in England is an estate agent. Estate agents represent the person selling their house or flat.

  In Scotland the process is different and you should go first to a solicitor. They both arrange for buyers to visit homes that are for sale.

- It is important that a solicitor helps you through the process of buying a house or flat. The solicitor will provide the legal agreements necessary for you to buy the property.

Renting accommodation

- Accommodation can be rented from the local authority (the council), from a housing association or from private property owners called landlords.

- Everyone is entitled to apply for council accommodation but in many areas of the UK there is a shortage of council accommodation, and that some people have to wait a very long time for a house or flat. You are then assessed according to your needs. This is done through a system of points. You get more points if you have priority needs, for example if you are homeless and have children or chronic ill health.

- When you rent a house or flat privately you sign a tenancy agreement or lease which explains the conditions or ?rules? you must follow while renting the property.

- The agreement also contains a list of any furniture or fittings in the property. Before you sign the agreement, check the details and keep it safe during your tenancy.

- You will probably be asked to give the landlord a deposit at the beginning of your tenancy. This is to cover the cost of any damage. It is usually equal to one month's rent. The landlord must return this money to you at the end of your tenancy, unless you have caused damage to the property.

Homelessness

- If you are homeless you should go for help to the local authority (or, in Northern Ireland, the Housing Executive). They have a legal duty to offer help and advice, but will not offer you a place to live unless you have priority need (see above) and have a connection with the area, such as work or family. You must also show that you have not made yourself intentionally homeless.

Water

- Water is supplied to all homes in the UK.
- The charge for this is called the water rates which can be paid in one payment (a lump sum) or in instalments, usually monthly.

Recycling your waste

- In many places you must recycle your rubbish, separating paper, glass, metal or plastic from the other rubbish. Large objects which you want to throw away, such as a bed, a wardrobe or a fridge, need to be collected separately.
- It is a criminal offence to dump rubbish anywhere.

Council Tax

- Local government services, such as education, police, roads, refuse collection and libraries, are paid for partly by grants from the government and partly by Council Tax.
- The amount of Council Tax you pay depends on the size and value of your house or flat (dwelling).

What to do if you have problems with your neighbours

- If you do have problems with your neighbours, they can usually be solved by speaking to them first. If you cannot solve the problem, speak to your landlord, local authority or housing association. Keep a record of the problems in case you have to show exactly what the problems are and when they started. Neighbours who cause a very serious nuisance may be taken to court and can be evicted from their home.

Opening a bank or building society account

- To open an account you need to show documents to prove your identity, such as a passport, immigration document or driving licence. You also need to show something with your address on it like a tenancy agreement or household bill.

Credit cards

- Credit cards can be used to buy things in shops, on the telephone and over the internet. Credit cards do not draw money from your bank account but you will be sent a bill every month. If you do not pay the total amount on the bill, you are charged interest.

Debit cards

- A debit card allows you to pay for things without using cash, but you must have enough money in your bank account to cover what you buy.

Store cards

- A store card also allows you to pay for things without using cash but it can only be used in a specific shop. Store cards do not draw money from your bank account but you will be sent a bill every month. If you do not pay the total amount on the bill, you will be charged interest.

Credit union

- Credit unions are financial co-operatives owned and controlled by their members. The members pool their savings and then make loans from this pool. Interest rates in credit unions are usually lower than banks and building societies.

Insurance

- Many people insure their property, possessions, credit cards and mobile phones. They also buy insurance when they travel abroad in case they lose their luggage or need medical treatment. Insurance is compulsory if you have a car or motorcycle.

Benefits

- Benefits are usually available for the sick and disabled, older people, the unemployed and those on low incomes. Guides to benefits are available from Jobcentre Plus offices, local libraries, post offices and the Citizens Advice Bureau.

Finding a doctor

- Family doctors are called General Practitioners (GPs) and they work in surgeries.
- Your GP is responsible for organising the health treatment you receive.
- You should look for a GP as soon as you move to a new area.
- You can get a list of local GPs from libraries, post offices, the tourist information office, the Citizens Advice Bureau, the local Health Authority and from the following websites:
- www.nhs.uk/ for health practitioners in England;
- www.wales.nhs.uk/directory.cfm for health practitioners in Wales;
- www.n-i.nhs.uk for health practitioners in Northern Ireland;
- www.show.scotnhs.uk/findnearest/healthservices in Scotland.

What to do if you feel unwell

- If you or your child feels unwell you have the following options:
- For information or advice
- Ask your local pharmacist (chemist). The pharmacy can give advice on medicines and some illnesses and conditions that are not serious
- Speak to a nurse by phoning NHS Direct on 0845 4647
- Use the NHS Direct website, NHS Direct Online: www.nhsdirect.nhs.uk

To see a doctor or nurse

- Make an appointment to see your GP or a nurse working in the surgery
- Visit an NHS walk-in centre.

For urgent medical treatment

- Contact your GP
- Go to your nearest hospital with an Accident and Emergency department
- Call 999 for an ambulance. Calls are free. ONLY use this service for a real emergency.

Dentists

- You can get the name of a dentist by asking at the local library, at the Citizens Advice Bureau and through NHS Direct

Opticians

- Most people have to pay for sight tests and glasses, except children, people over 60, people with certain eye conditions and people receiving certain benefits. In Scotland, eye tests are free.

Prescriptions

- Prescriptions are free for anyone who is
- Under 16 years of age (under 25 in Wales)
- Under 19 and in full-time education
- Aged 60 or over
- Pregnant or with a baby under 12 months old
- Suffering from a specified medical condition
- Receiving Income Support jobseekers' Allowance, Working Families or Disabilities Tax Credit

When it is possible to attend A & E without a doctor letter

- For urgent medical treatment
- If you are very ill out of your Doctors surgery hours or have had an accident, go to your nearest hospital with an Accident and Emergency department.

Dialing 999 or 112

- In extreme emergencies, call 999 for an ambulance. Calls are free. ONLY use this service for a real emergency.

NHS Direct

- NHS Direct Online is a website providing information about health services and several medical conditions and treatments: www.nhsdirect.nhs.uk

Pregnancy

- You can get information on maternity and ante-natal services in your area from your local health authority, a health visitor or your GP. The number of your health authority will be in the phone book.

Registering a birth

- Your must register your baby with the Registrar of Births, Marriages and Deaths (Register Office) within six weeks of the birth. The address of your local Register Office is in the phone book.

Education

- In England and Wales the primary stage lasts from 5 to 11, in Scotland from 5 to 12 and in Northern Ireland from 4 to 11.
- The secondary stage lasts until the age of 16. At that age young people can choose to leave school or to continue with their education until they are 17 or 18.

Types of School

- Education at state schools in the UK is free.
- Some primary and secondary schools in the UK are linked to the Church of England or the Roman Catholic Church. These are called 'faith schools'. In some areas there are Muslim, Jewish and Sikh schools.
- Independent schools are private schools. They are not run or paid for by the state. Independent secondary schools are also sometimes called public schools.

The National Curriculum

- All state, primary and secondary schools in England, Wales and Northern Ireland follow the National Curriculum. This covers English, maths, science, design and technology, information and communication technology (ICT), history, geography, modern foreign languages, art and design, music, physical education (PE) and citizenship.

Education for young people at the age of 16

- In England, at 16 they usually take the General Certificates of Secondary Education (GCSEs) in several subjects, although some schools also offer other qualifications.
- In Scotland, after 16 they can study at Intermediate, Higher or Advanced level.

Further Education colleges

- At 16, young people can leave school or stay on to do A levels (Higher grades in Scotland) in preparation for university.
- Some young people go to their local further education (FE) college to improve their exam grades or to get new qualifications for a career.
- Most courses are free up to the age of 19.
- Young people from families with low incomes can get financial help with their studies when they leave school at 16.

- Further education colleges also offer courses to adults over the age of 18.
- Classes are very varied and range from sports to learning a musical instrument or a new language.

ESOL (English for Speakers of Other Languages)

- People wishing to improve their skills in English can attend ESOL (English for Speakers of Other Languages) courses.
- There is sometimes a waiting list for ESOL courses because demand is high.
- You can get information at your local college or local library or from learndirect on 0800 100 900.

School governing bodies

- The governing body decides how the school is run and administered and produces reports on the progress of the school from year to year.
- In Scotland, parents can be members of school boards or parent councils.

Film classification

- Films are classified.
- U (Universal): suitable for anyone aged 4 years and over
- PG (parental guidance): suitable for everyone but some parts of the film might be unsuitable for children.
- 12 or 12a: children under 12 are not allowed to see or rent the film unless they are with an adult
- 15: children under 15 are not allowed to see or rent the film.
- 18: no one under l8is allowed to see or rent the film.
- R18: no one under 18 is allowed to see the film, which is only available in specially licensed cinemas.

Television licence

- Anyone in the UK with a television (TV), DVD or video recorder, computer or any device which is used for watching or recording TV programmes must be covered by a valid television licence.

Alcohol

- To drink alcohol in a pub you must be 18 or over.
- People under 18 are not allowed to buy alcohol in a supermarket or in an off-licence.

Driving licence

- You must have a driving licence to drive on public roads.
- You get a full driving licence in three stages:
  1. Apply for a provisional licence. You need this licence while you are learning to drive. With this you are allowed to drive a motorcycle up to 125cc or a car. You must put L plates on the vehicle, or D plates in Wales. Learner drivers cannot drive on a motorway. If you drive a car, you must be with someone who is over 21 and who has had a full licence for over three years. You can get an application form for a provisional licence from a post office.
  2. Pass a written theory test.
  3. Pass a practical driving test

Vehicle Insurance

- It is illegal to use your car if you not insured to drive it.

Road tax and MOT

- Your vehicle must display a valid road tax disc before you can drive it.
- If your vehicle is over three years old, you must have an MOT certificate.

Road accidents

- If you are involved in a road accident

- Don't drive away without stopping – this is a criminal offence
- Call the police and ambulance on 999 or 112 if someone is injured
- Get the names, addresses, vehicle registration numbers and insurance details of the other drivers
- Give your details to the other drivers or passengers and to the police
- Make a note of everything that happened and contact your insurance company as soon as possible.

Proving your identity

- Documents that prove your identity include:
- Official documents from the Home Office showing your immigration status
- A certificate of identity
- A passport or travel document
- A National Insurance (NI) number card
- A provisional or full driving licence
- A recent gas, electricity or phone bill showing your name and address
- A rent or benefits book.

Chapter 6 — EMPLOYMENT

Looking for work

If you are looking for work, or you are thinking of changing your job, there are a number of ways you can find out about work opportunities.

The Home Office provides guidance on who is allowed to work in the UK. Not everyone in the UK is allowed to work and some people need work permits, so it is important to check your status before taking up work. Also, employers have to check that anyone they employ is legally entitled to work in the UK. For more information and guidance, see the Home Office website 'Working in the UK' — www.workingintheuk.gov.uk

Jobs are usually advertised in local and national newspapers, at the local Jobcentre and in employment agencies. You can find the address and telephone number of your local Jobcentre under Jobcentre Plus in the phone book or see: www.jobcentreplus.gov.uk. Some jobs are advertised on supermarket notice boards and in shop windows. These jobs are usually part-time and the wages are often quite low. If there are particular companies you would like to work for, you can look for vacancies on their websites.

Jobcentre Plus is run by a government department — the Department for Work and Pensions. Trained staff give advice and help in finding and applying for jobs as well claiming benefits. They can also arrange for interpreters. Their website www.jobcentreplus.gov.uk lists vacancies and training opportunities and gives general information on benefits. There is also a low cost telephone service — Jobseeker Direct 0845 606 0234. This is open 9 a.m. to 6 p.m. on weekdays and 9 a.m. to 1 p.m. on Saturdays.

Qualifications

Applicants for some jobs need special training or qualifications. If you have qualifications from another country, you can find out how they compare with qualifications in the UK at the National Academic Recognition Information Centre (NARIC), www.naric.org.uk

For further information contact UK NARIC, ECCTIS Ltd, Oriel House, Oriel Road, Cheltenham Glos, GL5O 1XP telephone: 0870 990 4088, email: info@naric.org.uk

When you are applying for a job and during the interview, it is important to be honest about your qualifications and experience. If an employer later finds out that you gave incorrect information, you might lose your job.

Applications

Interviews for lower paid and local jobs can often be arranged by telephone or in person. For many jobs you need to fill in an application form or send a copy of your curriculum vitae (CV) with a covering letter or letter of application.

A covering letter is usually a short letter attached to a completed application form, while a letter of application gives more detailed information on why you are applying for the job and why you think you are suitable. Your CV gives specific details on your education, qualifications, previous employment skills and interests. It is important to type any letters and your CV on a computer or word processor as this improves your chance of being called for an interview.

Employers often ask for the names and addresses of one or two referees. These are people such as your current or previous employer or college tutor. Referees need to know you well and to agree to write a short report or reference on your suitability for the job. Personal friends or members of your family are not normally acceptable as referees.

Interviews

In job descriptions and interviews, employers should give full details of what the job involves, including the pay, holidays and working conditions. If you need more information about any of these, you can ask questions in the interview. In fact asking some questions in the interview shows you are interested and can improve your chance of getting the job.

Criminal record

For some jobs, particularly if the work involves working with children or vulnerable people, the employer will ask for your permission to do a criminal record check. You can get more information on this from the Home Office Criminal Records Bureau (CRB) information line, telephone 0870 909 0811. In Scotland, contact Disclosure Scotland: www.disclosurescotland.co.uk Helpline: 0870 6096006.

Training

Taking up training helps people improve their qualifications for work. Some training may be offered at work or you can do courses from home or at your local college. This includes English language training. You can get more information from your local library and college or from websites such as www.worktrain.gov.uk and www.learndirect.co.uk. Learndirect offers a range of online training courses at centres across the country. There are charges for courses but you can do free starter or taster sessions. You can get more information from their free information and advice line: 0800 100 900.

Volunteering and work experience

Some people do voluntary work and this can be a good way to support your local community and organisations which depend on volunteers. It also provides useful experience that can help with future job applications. Your local library will have information about volunteering opportunities.

Equal rights and discrimination

You can also get information and advice from websites such as: www.do-it.org.uk, www.volunteering.org.uk and www.justdosomething.net. It is against the law for employers to discriminate against someone at work. This means that a person should not be refused work, training or promotion or treated less favourably because of their

• sex

- nationality, race, colour or ethnic group

- disability

- religion

- sexual orientation

- age

In Northern Ireland, the law also bans discrimination on grounds of religious belief or political opinion.

The law also says that men and women who do the same job, or work of equal value, should receive equal pay. Almost all the laws protecting people at work apply equally to people doing part-time or full-time jobs.

There are, however a small number of jobs where discrimination laws do not apply. For example, discrimination is not against the law when the job involves working for someone in their own home.

You can get more information about the law and racial discrimination from the Commission for Racial Equality. The Equal Opportunities Commission can help with sex discrimination issues and the Disability Rights Commission deals with disability issues. Each of these organisations offers advice and information and can, in some cases, support individuals. From October 2007 their functions will be brought together in a new Commission for Equality and Human Rights. You can get more information about the laws protecting people at work from the Citizens Advice Bureau website: www.adviceguide.org.uk

In Northern Ireland, the Equality Commission provides information and advice in respect of all forms of unlawful discrimination.

The Commission for Racial Equality, St Dunstan House, 201-211 Borough High Street London, SE1 1GZ, telephone: 020 7939 000, fax: 020 7939 0001, www.cre.gov.uk

The Equal Opportunities Commission, Arndale House, Arndale Centre, Manchester M4 3EQ, telephone: 0845 601 5901, fax: 0161 8388312, www.eoc.org.uk

The Disability Rights Commission, DRC Helpline, FREEPOST MID02164, Stratford upon Avon CV37 9BR, telephone: 08457 622 633, fax: 08457 778 878, www.drc.org.uk

The Equality Commission for Northern Ireland, Equality House, 7-9 Shaftesbury Square, Belfast BT2 7DP, telephone: 02890500600, www.equalityni.org

Sexual harassment

Sexual harassment can take different forms. This includes:

- indecent remarks

- comments about the way you look that make you feel uncomfortable or humiliated

- comments or questions about your sex life

- inappropriate touching or sexual demands

- bullying behaviour or being treated in a way that is rude, hostile, degrading or humiliating because of your sex

Men and women can be victims of sexual harassment at work. If this happens to you, tell a friend, colleague or trade union representative and ask the person harassing you to stop. It is a good idea to keep a written record of what happened, the days and times when it happened and who else may have seen or heard the harassment. If the problem continues, report the person to your employer or trade union. Employers are responsible for the behaviour of their employees while they are at work. They should treat complaints of sexual harassment very seriously and take effective action to deal with the problem. If you are not satisfied with your employers response, you can ask for advice and support from the Equal Opportunities Commission, your trade union or the Citizens Advice Bureau.

At work

Both employers and employees have legal responsibilities at work. Employers have to pay employees for the work that they do, treat them fairly and take responsible care for their health and safety. Employees should do their work with reasonable skill and care and follow all reasonable instructions. They should not damage their employer's business.

A written contract or statement

Within two months of starting a new job, your employer should give you a written contract or statement with all the details and conditions for your work. This should include your responsibilities, pay, working hours, holidays, sick pay and pension. It should also include the period of notice that both you and your employer should give for the employment to end. The contract or written statement is an important document and is very useful if there is ever a disagreement about your work, pay or conditions.

Pay, hours and holidays

Your pay is agreed between you and your employer. There is a minimum wage in the UK that is a legal right for every employed person above compulsory school leaving age. The compulsory school leaving age is 16, but the time in the school year when 16-year-olds can leave school in England and Wales is different from that in Scotland and Northern Ireland.

There are different minimum wage rates for different age groups. From October 2006 the rates are as follows:

for workers aged 22 and above £5.35 an hour
for 18-21 year olds — £4.45 an hour
for 16-17 year olds — £3.30 an hour.

Employers who pay their workers less than this are breaking the law. You can get more information from the Central Office of Information Directgov website, www.direct.gov.uk which has a wide range of public service information. Alternatively, you can telephone the National Minimum Wage Helpline, telephone: 0845 600 0678.

Your contract or statement will show the number of hours you are expected to work. Your employer might ask you if you can work more hours than this and it is your decision whether or not you do. Your employer cannot require you to work more hours than the hours agreed on your contract

If you need to be absent from work, for example if you are ill or you have a medical appointment it is important to tell your employer as soon as you can in advance. Most employees who are 16 or over are entitled to at least four weeks, paid holiday every year. This includes time for national holidays (see chapter 3). Your employer must give you a pay slip, or a similar written statement each time you are paid. This must show exactly how much money has been taken off for tax and national insurance contributions.

Tax

For most people, tax is automatically taken from their earnings by the employer and paid directly to HM Revenue and Customs, the government department responsible for collecting taxes. If you are self-employed, you need to pay your own tax. Money raised from income tax pays for government services such as roads, education, police and the armed forces. Occasionally HM Revenue and Customs sends out tax return forms which ask for full financial details. If you receive one, it is important to complete it and return the form as soon as possible. You can get help and advice from the HM Revenue and Customs self-assessment helpline, on: 0845 300 45 55.

National Insurance

Almost everybody in the UK who is in paid work, including self-employed people, must pay National Insurance (NI) contributions. Money raised from NI contributions is used to pay contributory benefits such as the State Retirement Pension and helps fund the National Health Service. Employees have their NI contributions deducted from their pay by their employer every week or month. People who are self-employed need to pay NI contributions themselves: Class 2 contributions, either by direct debit or every three months and Class 4 contributions on the profits from their trade or business. Class 4 contributions are paid alongside their income tax. Anyone who does not pay enough NI contributions will not be able to receive certain benefits, such as Jobseekers Allowance or Maternity Pay, and may not receive a full state retirement pension.

Getting a National Insurance number

Just before their 16th birthday, all young people in the UK are sent a National Insurance number. This is a unique number for each person and it tracks their National Insurance contributions.

Refugees whose asylum applications have been successful have the same rights to work as any other UK citizen and to receive a National Insurance number. People who have applied for asylum and have not received a positive decision do not usually have permission to work and so do not get a National Insurance number.

You need a National Insurance number when you start work. If you do not have a National Insurance number, you can apply for one through Jobcentre Plus or your local Social Security Office. It is a good idea to make an appointment by telephone and ask which documents you need to take with you. You usually need to show your birth certificate, passport and Home Office documents allowing you to stay in the country. If you need information about registering for a National Insurance number, you can telephone the National Insurance Registrations Helpline on 084591 57006 or 0845 91 55670.

Pensions

Everyone in the UK who has paid enough National Insurance contributions will get a State Pension when they retire. The State Pension age for men is currently 65 years of age and for women it is 60, but the State Pension age for women will increase to 65 in stages between 2010 and 2020. You can find full details of the State Pension scheme on the State Pension website, www.thepensionservice.gov.uk or you can phone the Pension Service Helpline: 0845 606 0265.

In addition to a State Pension, many people also receive a pension through their work and some also pay into a personal pension plan too. It is very important to get good advice about pensions. The Pensions Advisory Service gives free and confidential advice on occupational and personal pensions. Their helpline telephone number is 0845 601 2923 and their website address is www.opas.org.uk. Independent financial advisers can also give advice but you usually have to pay a fee for this service. You can find local financial advisers in the Yellow Pages and Thomson local guides or on the internet at www.unbiased.co.uk

Health and safety

Employers have a legal duty to make sure the workplace is safe. Employees also have a legal duty to follow safety regulations and to work safely and responsibly. If you are worried about health and safety at your workplace, talk to your supervisor, manager or trade union representative. You need to follow the right procedures and your employer must not dismiss you or treat you unfairly for raising a concern.

Trade unions

Trade unions are organisations that aim to improve the pay and working conditions of their members. They also give their members advice and support on problems at work. You can choose whether to join a trade union or not and your employer cannot dismiss you or treat you unfairly for being a union member.

You can find details of trade unions in the UK, the benefits they offer to members and useful information on rights at work on the Trades Union Congress (TUC) website, www.tuc.org.uk

Problems at work

If you have problems of any kind at work, speak to your supervisor manager, trade union representative or someone else with responsibility as soon as possible. If you need to take any action, it is a good idea to get advice first. If you are a member of a trade union, your representative will help. You can also contact your local Citizens Advice Bureau (CAB) or Law Centre. The national Advisory, Conciliation and Arbitration Service (ACAS) website, www.acas.org.uk gives information on your rights at work. ACAS also offers a national helpline, telephone: 0845 747 4747.

Losing your job and unfair dismissal

An employee can be dismissed immediately for serious misconduct at work. Anyone who cannot do their job properly, or is unacceptably late or absent from work, should be given a warning by their employer. If their work, punctuality or attendance does not improve, the employer can give them notice to leave their job.

It is against the law for employers to dismiss someone from work unfairly. If this happens to you, or life at work is made so difficult that you feel you have to leave, you may be able to get compensation if you take your case to an Employment Tribunal. This is a court which specialises in employment matters. You normally only have three months to make a complaint.

If you are dismissed from your job, it is important to get advice on your case as soon as possible. You can ask for advice and information on your legal rights and the best action to take from your trade union representative, a solicitor, a Law Centre or the Citizen's Advice Bureau.

Redundancy

If you lose your job because the company you work for no longer needs someone to do your job, or cannot afford to employ you, you may be entitled to redundancy pay. The amount of money you receive depends on the length of time you have been employed. Again your trade union representative, a solicitor, a Law Centre or the Citizens Advice Bureau can advise you.

Unemployment

Most people who become unemployed can claim Jobseeker's Allowance (JSA). This is currently available for men aged 18-65 and women aged 18-60 who are capable of working, available for work and trying to find work. Unemployed 16 and 17-year-olds may not be eligible for Jobseeker's Allowance but may be able to claim a Young Person's Bridging Allowance (YPBA) instead. The local Jobcentre Plus can help with claims. You can get further information from the Citizens Advice Bureau and the Jobcentre Plus website: www.jobcentreplus.gov.uk

New Deal

New Deal is a government programme that aims to give unemployed people the help and support they need to get into work. Young people who have been unemployed for 6 months and adults who have been unemployed for 18 months are usually required to join New Deal if they wish to continue receiving benefit. There are different New Deal schemes for different age groups. You can find out more about New Deal on 0845 606 2626 or: www.newdeal.gov.uk

The government also runs work-based learning programmes which offer training to people while they are at work. People receive a wage or an allowance and can attend college for one day a week to get a new qualification.

You can find out more about the different government schemes, and the schemes in your area, from Jobcentre Plus, www.jobcentreplus.gov.uk, or your local Citizens Advice Bureau.

Working for yourself

Tax

Self-employed people are responsible for paying their own tax and National Insurance. They have to keep detailed records of what they earn and spend on the business and send their business accounts to HM Revenue and Customs every year. Most self-employed people use an accountant to make sure they pay the correct tax and claim all the possible tax allowances.

As soon as you become self-employed you should register yourself for tax and National Insurance by ringing the HM Revenue and Customs telephone helpline for people who are self-employed, on 0845 915 4515.

Help and advice

Banks can give information and advice on setting up your own business and offer start-up loans, which need to be repaid with interest. Government grants and other financial support may be available. You can get details of these and advice on becoming self-employed from Business Link, a government-funded project for people starting or running a business: www.businesslink.gov.uk telephone: 0845 600 9006.

Working in Europe

British citizens can work in any country that is a member of the European Economic Area (EEA). In general, they have the same employment rights as a citizen of that country or state.

Childcare and children at work

New mothers and fathers

Women who are expecting a baby have a legal right to time off work for antenatal care. They are also entitled to at least 26 weeks' maternity leave. These rights apply to full-time and part-time workers and it makes no difference how long the woman has worked for her employer. It is, however, important to follow the correct procedures and to give the employer enough notice about taking maternity leave. Some women may also be entitled to maternity pay but this depends on how long they have been working for their employer.

Fathers who have worked for their employer for at least 26 weeks are entitled to paternity leave, which provides up to two weeks' time off from work, with pay, when the child is born. It is important to tell your employer well in advance.

You can get advice and more information on maternity and paternity matters from the personnel officer at work, your trade union representative, your local

Citizens Advice Bureau, the Citizens Advice Bureau website www.adviceguide.org.uk or the government website www.direct.gov.uk

Childcare

It is Government policy to help people with childcare responsibilities to take up work. Some employers can help with this. The ChildcareLink website www.childcarelink.gov.uk gives information about different types of childcare and registered childminders in your area, or telephone 0800 096 0296.

Hours and time for children at work

In the UK there are strict laws to protect children from exploitation and to make sure that work does not get in the way of their education. The earliest legal age for children to do paid work is set at 14. There are a few exceptions that allow children under the age of 14 to work legally and these include specific work in performing, modelling, sport and agriculture. In order to do any of this work, it is necessary to get a licence from the local authority.

By law, children aged 14 to 16 can only do light work. There are particular jobs they are not allowed to do and these include delivering milk, selling alcohol, cigarettes or medicines, working in a kitchen or a chip shop, working with dangerous machinery or doing any other kind of work that might cause them any kind of injury. Children who work have to get an employment card from their local authority and a medical certificate of fitness for work.

The law sets out clear limits for the working hours and times for 14-16 year-old children. Every child must have at least two consecutive weeks a year during the school holidays when they do not work. They cannot work:

- for more than 4 hours without a one-hour rest break

- for more than 2 hours on any school day or a Sunday before 7 a.m. or after 7 a.m.

- for more than one hour before school starts

- for more than 12 hours in any school week

15 and 16-year-olds can work slightly more hours than 14-year-olds on a weekday when they are not at school, on Saturdays and in school holidays.

The local authority has a duty to check that the law is obeyed. If it believes that a young person is working illegally, it can order that the young person is no longer employed. You can find more information on the TUC website, www.worksmartorg.uk

Chapter 6 — QuickStudy

Entitlement to work

- Not everyone in the UK is allowed to work and some people need work permits, so it is important to check your status before taking up work.

NARIC

- If you have qualifications from another country, you can find out how they compare with qualifications in the UK at the National Academic Recognition Information Centre (NARIC), www.naric.org.uk

CVs

- For many jobs you need to fill in an application form or send a copy of your curriculum vitae (CV) with a covering letter or letter of application. Your CV gives specific details on your education, qualifications, previous employment skills and interests.

- It is important to be honest about your qualifications and experience. If an employer later finds out that you gave incorrect information, you might lose your job.

Referees

- Employers often ask for the names and addresses of one or two referees. These are people such as your current or previous employer or college tutor. Personal friends or members of your family are not normally acceptable as referees.

Criminal record

- Some employers will ask for your permission to do a criminal record check. You can get more information on this from the Home Office Criminal Records Bureau (CRB) information line, telephone 0870 909 0811.

- In Scotland, contact Disclosure Scotland: www.disclosurescotland.co.uk Helpline: 0870 609 6006.

Training

- Training can help people improve their qualifications for work
- You can get more information from your local library and college or from websites such as www.worktrain.gov.uk and www.learndirect.co.uk or free information and advice line: 0800 100 900.

Job seeking

- Jobs are usually advertised in local and national newspapers, at the local Jobcentre and in employment agencies. Some jobs are advertised on supermarket notice boards and in shop windows. These jobs are usually part-time and the wages are often quite low.
- If there are particular companies you would like to work for, you can look for vacancies on their websites.
- Jobcentre Plus has trained staff that can give advice and help in finding and applying for jobs.

Volunteering

- Voluntary work can be a good way to support your local community and it can provide useful experience that can help with future job applications. You can also get information and advice from websites such as: www.do-it.org.uk www.volunteering.org.uk and wwwjustdosomething.net.

Equal rights

- It is against the law for employers to discriminate against someone at work on grounds of sex, nationality, race, colour or ethnic group, disability, religion and sexual orientation.
- There are a small number of jobs where discrimination laws do not apply. For example, discrimination is not against the law when the job involves working for someone in their own home.

Equal job/equal pay

- The law also says that men and women who do the same job, or work of equal value, should receive equal pay.

Equality commissions

- Further information on equality can be obtained from The Commission for Racial Equality, The Equal Opportunities Commission, The Disability Rights Commission and in Northern Ireland, The Equality Commission for Northern Ireland.

Sexual harassment

- Indecent remarks, comments about the way you look that make you feel uncomfortable or humiliated, comments or questions about your sex life, inappropriate touching or sexual demands, bullying behaviour or being treated in a way that is rude, hostile, degrading or humiliating because of your sex all constitute Sexual harassment and employers should treat complaints of sexual harassment very seriously and take effective action to deal with the problem.

Contracts of employment

- The contract or written statement is an important document and is very useful if there is ever a disagreement about your work, pay or conditions.

The minimum wage

- From October 2006 the rates are as follows:
  - for workers aged 22 and above £5.35 an hour

  - for 18-21 year olds – £4.45 an hour

  - for 16-17 year olds – £3.30 an hour.

- Employers who pay their workers less than this are breaking the law.

Holiday entitlement

- Most employees who are 16 or over are entitled to at least four weeks paid holiday every year including national holidays.

Pay slips

- Your employer must give you a pay slip each time you are paid. This must show exactly how much money has been taken off for tax and national insurance contributions.

Tax

- Most people have tax automatically deducted from their earnings by their employer and paid directly to the government. Taxes pay for government services such as roads, education, police and the armed forces.

Filling out tax forms

- You can get help and advice from the HM Revenue and Customs self-assessment helpline, on: 0845 300 45 55.

National Insurance

- Almost everybody in the UK who is in paid work must pay National Insurance (NI) contributions. NI contributions pay the State Retirement Pension and for the National Health Service. Anyone who does not pay enough NI contributions will not be able to receive certain benefits, such as Jobseekers Allowance or Maternity Pay, and may not receive a full state retirement pension

How you can get a National Insurance number

- Just before their 16th birthday, all young people in the UK are sent a National Insurance number. This is a unique number for each person and it tracks their National Insurance contributions

Pensions

- Everyone in the UK who has paid enough National Insurance contributions will get a State Pension when they retire. The State Pension age for men is currently 65 years of age and for women it is 60, but the State Pension age for women will increase to 65 in stages between 2010 and 2020.

You can find full details of the State Pension scheme on the State Pension website, www.thepensionservice.gov.uk.

Health and safety

- Employers have a legal duty to make sure the workplace is safe. Employees also have a legal duty to follow safety regulations and to work safely and responsibly. If you are worried about health and safety at your workplace, talk to your supervisor, manager or trade union representative.

Trade unions

- Trade unions are organisations that aim to improve the pay and working conditions of their members. They also give their members advice and support on problems at work. You can choose whether to join a trade union or not and your employer cannot dismiss you or treat you unfairly for being a union member.

- You can find details of trade unions in the UK, the benefits they offer to members and useful information on rights at work on the Trades Union Congress (TUC) website, www.tuc.org.uk.

Losing your job

- Anyone who cannot do their job properly, or is unacceptably late or absent from work, should be given a warning by their employer. If their work, punctuality or attendance does not improve, the employer can give them notice to leave their job.

- It is against the law for employers to dismiss someone from work unfairly. If this happens to you, or life at work is made so difficult that you feel you have to leave, you may be able to get compensation if you take your case to an Employment Tribunal.

- You normally only have three months to make a complaint.

- If you have problems of any kind at work, speak to your supervisor manager, trade union representative or someone else with responsibility as soon as possible. You can also contact your local Citizens Advice Bureau (CAB) or Law Centre.

- The national Advisory, Conciliation and Arbitration Service (ACAS) website, www.acas.org.uk gives information on your rights at work. ACAS also offers a national helpline, telephone: 0845 747 4747.

Redundancy

- If you lose your job because the company you work for no longer needs someone to do your job you may be entitled to redundancy pay. The amount of money you receive depends on the length of time you have been employed.

Self-employment

- Self-employed people are responsible for paying their own tax and National Insurance. They have to keep detailed records of what they earn and spend on the business and send their business accounts to HM Revenue and Customs every year. As soon as you become self-employed you should register yourself for tax and National Insurance by ringing the HM Revenue and Customs telephone helpline for people who are self-employed, on 0845 915 4515.

Business Link

- You can get advice on setting up your own business, start-up loans, government grants and other financial support from Business Link www.businesslink.gov.uk telephone: 0845 600 9006

Maternity rights

- Women who are expecting a baby have a legal right to time off work for antenatal care. They are also entitled to at least 26 weeks' maternity leave. These rights apply to full-time and part-time workers and it makes no difference how long the woman has worked for her employer. Some women may also be entitled to maternity pay but this depends on how long they have been working for their employer.
- It is important to follow the correct procedures and to give the employer enough notice about taking maternity leave.

Paternity rights

- Fathers who have worked for at least 26 weeks are entitled to paternity leave, which provides up to two weeks' time off from work, with pay, when the child is born. It is important to tell your employer well in advance.

Children at work

- The minimum legal age for children to do paid work is 14. Children aged 14 to 16 can only do light work. They cannot deliver milk, sell alcohol, cigarettes or medicines, work in a kitchen or a chip shop, work with dangerous machinery or do any other kind of work that might cause them any kind of injury.
- All children must have at least two consecutive weeks a year during the school holidays when they do not work.
- They cannot work:
    - for more than 4 hours without a one-hour rest break

    - for more than 2 hours on any school day or a Sunday before 7 a.m. or after 7 a.m.

    - for more than one hour before school starts

    - for more than 12 hours in any school week

- 15 and 16-year-olds can work slightly more hours than 14-year-olds on a weekday when they are not at school, on Saturdays and in school holidays.
- Children who work have to get an employment card from their local authority and a medical certificate of fitness for work.
- The local authority has a duty to check that the laws governing the employment of children are obeyed.

Notes

STUDY PROGRAM DETAILS

The Life in the UK Test consists of questions taken from chapters 2, 3, 4, 5 & 6.

This section describes how to use the quizzes contained on the CD in the back of this book. The interactive multiple choice question and answer quizzes can be used as part of a structured learning program, building your confidence as you progress.

- Read and study chapter 2 and then use the chapter 2 quiz which randomly selects a set of 24 questions from this chapter. You can repeat the test again and again each time generating a random selection of 24 questions.

  Once you are satisfied that you can confidently score more than 75% each time you run this quiz, then you can move on to studying chapters 3, 4, 5 and 6 using the related quizzes in the same manner.

- Once you feel that you have mastered chapters 2, 3, 4, 5 and 6, you can move onto the sixth quiz, which randomly selects a set of 24 questions from our extensive database of questions and answers based on chapters 2, 3, 4, 5 and 6. You can repeat this test again and again each time generating a random selection of 24 questions until you feel confident that you are ready for the Home Office test itself. You can use the chapter summaries at the end of each chapter to refresh your knowledge of the key points contained in each chapter.

- Finally, using the last test, you have the option of working through all of the questions in the same order as they appear in the book.

  Simply select the test you want to run and follow the instructions.

SOFTWARE LICENSE

The Interactive Multiple Choice Test Software Program attached to this book is Copyright material. It is not public domain. You are not permitted to extract, add to or copy the contents without the express written authority of the authors.

This software is provided "as-is," without any express or implied warranty. In no event shall the authors be held liable for any damages arising from the use of this software.

ABOUT THE AUTHORS

Paul Lancaster is a freelance software consultant with over 25 years experience presenting and developing computer-based training packages. Paul, although born in England, has spent most of his life living overseas. He lives in England with his wife, Mary-Ann and their Jack Russell terrier, Eddie.

Mary-Ann Coull was born in Johannesburg, South Africa and immigrated to Britain. She has passed through the UK immigration process herself. She works as a freelance webmaster, internet entrepreneur and author. In her spare time she enjoys yoga, aqua-fit and dog walking.

We appreciate your questions or feedback. You are welcome to contact the authors.

feedback@lancasterandcoull.co.uk

Notes

Quick Reference Glossary

This glossary will help you understand key words and expressions which have been used in this book. S/he is used to mean 'she or he'.

Absent from work	not at work, e.g. because of illness
Accountant	a person whose job is to keep business records, to work out how much money a person or business is making or losing, and how much business tax needs to be paid
Accents/dialects	regional differences in speech
Addictive substance	usually a type of drug that a person feels a strong need to take very often, and finds very difficult to stop using
Asylum	a place where people, who are accused of crime in another country, can live in safety
Asylum seekers	people who leave their own country because they feel it is too dangerous for them to stay there (usually because of political reasons) and who then formally ask to stay in another country where it will be safer for them to live
Bank Holiday	a day when most people have an official day off work and when banks and most other businesses are closed-a Bank Holiday can also be called a public holiday
Betting shop/gambling	a place where a person can go and pay to try to win money by gambling on the results of horse racing, football matches etc
Binge drinking	the consumption of dangerously large quantities of alcoholic beverages in one session
Birth certificate	an official document that states the name of a person, the place and date of his/her birth, and the names and occupations of his/her parents
Bishop	a senior priest in a Christian religion who is the head of different churches in a specified area
Bound, legally	obliged to do something in a way that follows certain laws
Building society	a kind of bank which can be used for saving money or for borrowing money from in order to buy a house
Built-up area	a place where there are a lot of buildings and not many open spaces and where a lot of people live and/or work
Bureaux de change	places where people can exchange one currency for another, e.g.

	they can sell pounds to buy euros
Business accounts	an official record of the amount of money a business is making, and how much it is paying for equipment etc, that is used to calculate the amount of tax that must be paid to the government
By-election	election which is held when an MP resigns or dies and when a new MP needs to be elected to replace him/her in Parliament before the next general election
Cabinet (government)	a group of senior ministers who are responsible for controlling government policy
Cable company	a company that can supply customers with a telephone or cable television connection
Carriageway(s)	a single carriageway is a road which is only wide enough for one lane of traffic and which is divided from another road which takes traffic going in the opposite direction
Census (government)	an official count of the number of people who live in a country and possibly including information about those people, e.g. age, race, marital status etc
Charity, give to	give money or take action to help people who are suffering from poverty, illnesses, starvation etc.
Charter (government)	an official written statement which describes the rights and responsibilities of a state and its citizens
Chief Whip	The Chief Whip has to maintain party discipline and to try to ensure that members of the party vote with the government in important debates.
Childminder	a person whose job it is to look after young children, usually while the children's parents are at work – a childminder usually has a qualification to do this kind of work
Citizens advice bureau	Helps people resolve their money, legal and other problems by providing information and advice
Civil service	the departments within government
Clamp (transport, police)	a metal device that is put on the wheel of a car to prevent it from being driven away (usually used because the car is parked somewhere illegally) – the driver will have to pay to have the clamp removed
Clarification (language)	a clear way of saying something that is easy to understand
Commemorate	do something to show that something is someone important is remembered, usually on a particular day

Commonwealth of Nations	an association of Britain and of sovereign states that used to be British colonies or states that are still ruled by Britain – the British monarch is accepted by the Commonwealth countries as their ruler
Community events	events which are organized within a local area to help, in some way, the people who live or work in the same area, e.g. a town might hold a community event in order to raise money to buy special equipment for a local school
Compensation (money)	money which must be paid to someone because they have suffered in some way e.g. loss, injury. compensation can also be part of a person if their employer has treated them unfairly or illegally
Compulsory testing	tests which must be done by law
Concern	worry about an important problem / a worrying thing
Confidential information	information that is private and secret and only known to the giver and receiver of that information
Consecutive	following one another without a break or interruption, e.g. next week we must have meetings on consecutive days, Tuesday and Wednesday
Constituency	a specific area where the voters who live in that place (its constituents) can elect an MP to represent them in Parliament
Constitution	the legal structure of established laws and principles which is used to govern a country
Contraception	methods used to prevent women who have sex from becoming pregnant, e.g. taking contraceptive pills, using a condom
Contributions	money paid regularly by someone which will help pay for something which is worth much more, e.g. a pension
Convention	an official agreement, usually between countries, about particular rules or codes of behaviour
Credit card	a card which a person can use to buy goods or services which are paid for by a credit company-the credit company then sends the card-holder a monthly bill-goods can therefore be bought, but paid for later
Criminal	a person who is found guilty of breaking the law
Criminal offence	an illegal activity, burglary, for which the criminal may be prosecuted
Currency (money)	a particular system of money that a country or group of countries use, e.g. in the EU, the form of currency that is used most widely is

	the euro
Cut off (service)	disconnect the supply of something
Debate	a discussion in which people give different opinions, about something/to discuss and give different opinions about something
Debit card	a card which a person can use to buy goods or services with money that is in their bank or building society account-the money is taken from their account automatically
Defeat	to be stronger than an opponent and therefore win a battle, a war, a competition etc.
Democratic country	a country which is governed by people who are elected by the population to represent them in Parliament
Dentist	Someone who looks after your teeth
Deposit (housing)	an amount of money paid to a landlord when a person rents a flat or house — this money is given back when the person leaves, but only if the property or furniture has not been damaged
Descent, of	coming originally from, e.g. of Indian descent means being a member of a family coming originally from India
Devolution/devolving	the passing of power from a central government to another group at a regional or local level which can then be called a devolved administration
Dialect	form of a language which is spoken only by a particular social group or a group of people living in a particular area
Direct debit	an arrangement that a person makes to transfer an amount of money from his/her bank account into another account on a regular basis
Disability, physical/mental	a condition that a person has that makes doing ordinary things like walking, seeing, speaking, talking, or learning difficulties
Discrimination	the act of treating an individual or a particular group of people in a way which is unfair, for example because of their race, nationality, sex, sexuality, age, or disability. Paying a woman less than a man for the same work is an example of discrimination
Dismissal (employment)	removal from a job, the 'sack'
Disputes	arguments or disagreements that are serious and about which people may take legal advice or action
Divorce	the legal end of a marriage/the act of ending a marriage

Doctor	one who looks after a person's health
Domestic rates	a type of tax in Northern Ireland which is paid by residents to their local authority and which helps to pay for local services, e.g. education, road repairs, policing, refuse collection
Driving licence	a permit to drive a motor vehicle
dual carriageway	is a road which is wide enough for two lanes of traffic and which is divided from another road which takes traffic in the opposite direction
Dump	get rid of something, throw away — often in a place where rubbish should not be left/a place where rubbish is left in an untidy and unhealthy way
Dwelling	a place where people live, e.g. a house, a flat
Education	schooling or training
Elections	The act or power of electing someone to office
Electoral register	the official list of all the people in a country who are allowed to vote in an election
Electricity	supplied by different suppliers for power and heating in the home
Eligible	allowed by law
Emergency services	services that can be telephoned and that will come to the help of people when they need it quickly and very urgently, e.g. the police service, fire service, ambulance service, coastguard service and, at sea, the lifeguard service
Employ	give someone work and pay them to do it
Employee	someone who is paid by an employer to do a job
Employer	a person or company that gives work to other people and pays them for doing it
Entitled (law)	officially allowed (to do something)
Estate agent	a person whose job is to sell houses and land
Euro	the official common currency of 12 European Union nations
Ethnic minority	group of people who are of a different race from the race of the majority of the population in a particular
European Commission	the executive group of the European Union that initiates action and safeguards the EU nations
European Union (EU)	a political and economical association of European countries which encourages trade and cooperation between its member states
Evict (housing)	order someone legally to leave the house where they are living

Evidence, collecting	looking for and getting information, documents or items that show for certain that something has happened, e.g. the police went to the criminals house to collect as much evidence as possible
Exchange rate	the amount of money in one currency that you need to buy a certain amount of money in another currency, e.g. £1 = $1.9 The exchange rate can vary from day to day
Exploitation	situation in which someone is made to do something unfairly because they are given nothing or very little for doing it, e.g. the women were exploited by their employer who paid them less than the minimum wage and also forced them to work overtime
Faith school	some primary and secondary schools in the UK are linked to a particular faith
Famine	a situation in which there is very little food for a long time and people often die because of this
First past the post	a system of election In which the candidate with the largest number of votes in a particular constituency wins a seat in Parliament
Flooding (housing)	water coming inside a property (and which probably causes damage to it)
Free press	newspapers and other reporting that are not controlled by government and can therefore write freely without restriction, about anything they think their readers will be interested in
Further education	some young people go to their local further education (FE) college to improve their exam grades or to get new qualifications for a career
Gambling (money)	risking money to try to win more money, e.g, in card games or by trying to guess the winner of a horse race or football match
Gap year (education)	a year between leaving school and going to university during which many students choose to gain experience through travelling, or to earn money by taking a job
Gas	gas is supplied by different suppliers for fuel and heating in the home
General election	a situation in which all the citizens of a country who are allowed to vote choose the people they wish to represent them in their government-in Britain this usually happens every five years
Government policies	official ideas and beliefs that are agreed by a political party about how to govern the country

Grant (money)	an amount of money paid by an authority to help a person or organisation pay for a particular thing, e,g. education course, a business expansion
Harassment (behaviour)	rude, offensive, threatening or bullying behaviour - a word often used to describe this kind of behaviour in a workplace
Hard drugs	drugs which are illegal and are very powerful and addictive
Health authority, local	an organisation which manages health care and from which people and get advice about where to find medical
Health hazards	things that might be dangerous to someone's health, e.g. Smoking is a hazard to health because it can cause lung cancer
Heir	someone who will legally receive another person's money, property, possessions or position when that person dies
Helmet	hard hat that protects the head against injury - a crash helmet must be worn by someone who is riding a motorcycle
Heroin	type of drug which is addictive, powerful and illegal
Higher education	education that students receive at college or university
Homelessness	Without any place to stay/live
House of Commons	that part of the Houses of Parliament where MPs who are elected by the voting public debate political issues
House of Lords	that part of the Houses of Parliament where the people who have inherited seats or been especially chosen by the Prime Minister debate political issues
Household	the home and the people who live in it/something that relates to the home, e.g. household chores are jobs that need to be done in the home like cleaning and cooking
Houses of Parliament	the building in London which comprises the House of Commons, the House of Lords and other offices where the British Parliament meets, debates and passes laws
Housing	places for people to stay/live in
Housing association	independent not-for-profit organisations which provide housing for rent
Humiliated	feel ashamed, stupid or embarrassed because of something that happens to you, usually when other people are there
Immigration	enter another country to live and work there, someone who does this is an Immigrant
Inappropriate touching	touching someone on a part of his/her body or in a way that is offensive and not acceptable in a particular situation

Indecent remarks	something that is said that contains words which are rude, sexual and offensive
Independent school	independent schools are private schools. They are not run or paid for by the state
Independents (politics)	MPs who do not represent any of the main political parties
Innocent (law)	found by a court NOT to be responsible for committing a crime
In-patient	someone who needs medical care and needs to stay in hospital overnight or longer
Instalments (money)	a series of equal payments which are paid regularly over a period of time until the total cost of something is paid, e.g. a person may pay for a TV that costs £200 in ten monthly instalments of £20
Insure	pay money to an insurance company in case e.g. a car or property is damaged — if this happens, the insurance company will help to pay for repairs
Intentionally	on purpose, deliberately
Interest (money)	extra money that must be paid to a lender when someone borrows money — this is usually calculated as a percentage of the loan — if the interest rate is 10% and the person borrows £100, the interest that must be paid on the loan will be an extra £10
Interpreter	a person whose job is to change something that is spoken or written in one language into another language without changing the meaning
Islamic mortgage/Sharia	loan for buying a house, and when the person who receives the loan only needs to pay back the original sum — no extra money needs to be paid
Judge (law)	the most important official in court whose job is to make sure that court proceedings are lawful and fair, and to decide which punishment to give a criminal if s/he is found guilty by the court
Judiciary	all the judges in a country who, together, are responsible for using the law of the land in the correct way
Jury	ordinary people (usually a group of 12 people) who listen to information and then decide whether someone is guilty or innocent in a court of law
Landlord, landlady (housing)	a man (landlord) or woman (landlady) who owns a house or flat and rents it to people (tenants) who must pay them money (rent) to live there
Legal	allowed to do by law or must do by law

Leisure centre	a building where people can go and pay to do sports indoors, e.g. swimming, badminton
Letting agent	a service which helps landlords find tenants and tenants find places to rent see
Life Peers	members of the House of Lords
Lord Chancellor	The Minister responsible for legal affairs
Magistrate	a person who acts as a judge in a court case where the crime is not as serious as some others
Mainland	an area of land which forms a country and does not include any of its surrounding islands
Marital status	information about whether a person is single, married, separated or divorced that is often asked for on official
Maternity leave	time allowed off work for a woman during her pregnancy and after her baby is born and during which time she usually continues to receive a wage
Maternity services	medical and social help relating to motherhood from early pregnancy until after the baby has been born
Media	all the organisations that give information to the public, e.g. newspapers, magazines, television, radio and the internet
Mediation	advice and support given by a person or organisation to end an argument between two other people or group if people who cannot agree about something
Mental illness	an illness in which a person appears to behave or think in ways that are not considered to be normal, e.g. depression is a mental illness that makes people feel unnecessarily sad, worried or frightened and can prevent them from doing routine things like shopping, having fun with friends etc.
Meter (housing)	machine that shows, in units or numbers how much electricity, gas or water has been used In a household the number on a meter that shows how much electricity, gas or water has been used
Migrate (people)	move to another country to live and work there — someone who does this is a migrant
Misuse	use something in a wrong way or for a wrong reason
Molestation	a sexual attack on someone (often a child)
Monarch	the king or queen of a country
Mortgage	a loan, usually from a building society or bank, that is used to buy or help buy a house or flat — the loan Is usually paid back in

	instalments over a number of years
Motor (transport)	a machine that makes something move/a car
MP	Member of Parliament — the person who is elected by his or her constituents to represent them in government
Naturalised citizen	someone who is born in one country but becomes a citizen of another country
NHS	National Health Service
Not-for-profit	a way of doing business in which an organisation or company will not try to make any money from providing their service or goods
Notice (employment)	a length of time that an employee must continue to work after telling an employer that s/he wants to leave the job/a length of time that an employer must continue to employ someone after asking her/him to leave, e.g. my boss only gave me one week's notice so I was really upset
Notice, to give	to give someone information about something that is going to happen in the future that will change a situation
Nuisance (behaviour)	something that annoys or causes problems for other people
Office, to be in	to be in power in government
Off-licence	a shop that sells alcohol in bottles or cans, e.g. wine, beer
Online	on the internet
On-the-spot fines	an immediate demand for money which must be paid as a punishment for doing something wrong, e.g. to receive an on-the-spot fine for driving too fast
Opposition	the second largest party that is not in power in the government, e.g. in 2006, the Labour Party was in power and the Conservatives were in Opposition and David Cameron was the Leader of the Opposition
Optician	An optician is an eye care professional who provides lenses for the correction of vision defects
Outpatient	someone who needs medical care in a hospital but does not need to stay overnight
Party politics	the shared and particular ideas and beliefs of an organised group of politicians, e.g. the Labour Party
Paternity leave	time allowed off work for a man whose wife or partner is going to have a baby or has just had a baby and during which time he usually continues to receive a wage
Patient (medical)	someone whom a doctor looks after or who need medical care

	because they are ill, have an injury etc
Patron Saint	Christian Saint who, according to religious belief protects a particular place or a particular group of people
Peers	members of the House of Lords
Penalty (law)	punishment for breaking the law, e.g. a fine
Pension plan, pay into a	to save money regularly while a person is working so that when a person stops going to work at 60 or older there will be enough money to provide him/her with a pension
Performing (theatre)	acting or dancing
Permit (law)	a document that allows someone to legally do something, e.g. a work permit
Personal details	information about a person that can be used to identify them, e.g. their name, date of birth, address, marital status etc.
Personnel officer	someone whose job in a company is to employ staff and to help solve problems that employees have at work
Phonecard, pre-paid	a card that can be bought and then used to make a certain number of phone calls up to the value of the card
PIN number	four numbers which have to be tapped into a cash machine if someone wants to withdraw money from their account or pay for something using credit or debit cards. Using a personal identification number (PIN) stops other people from using cards if they are stolen so the numbers must be remembered and kept secret
Pocket money	a small amount of money that a parent might give to his/her child on a regular basis, e.g. once a week, so that the child can buy his/her own comics or sweets etc.
Pogroms	the intentional killing of many people usually because of their race or religious belief
Possessions	things that people own, e.g. a car, clothes, a television, books
Pregnancy	the nine-month period before birth during which a baby grows inside its mother - the mother is pregnant at this time
Prescription (medical)	a note from a doctor saying which medicines a patient needs
Pressure group	a group of people who try to persuade the government to do something or to persuade the public to change their opinion about something
Primary school	mixed medium school (for both boys and girls) up to age of 11
Prime Minister	the Member of Parliament who is the leader of the political party in

	power and therefore of the whole government
Promotion (employment)	movement to a better or to a more important job within the same company, e.g. she was promoted from shop assistant to sales manageress
Proof	information, items, documents etc. that show that something has definitely happened
Proportional representation	a system of election in which political parties are allowed a number of seats in Parliament that represents their share of the total number of votes cast
Pub	public house — a place where adults over the age of 18 can buy and drink alcohol
Public body	a governmental department or a group of people who represent or work for the government and work for the good of the general public
Public order	a situation where rules are obeyed in a public place
Public place	place which is not private and where ordinary people can spend time together, or on their own, e.g. a cinema, a restaurant, a library, pub, a park
Punctual	arriving at the right time, not being late for something, e.g. work or a doctor's appointment
Racial	relating to race, e.g. racial discrimination
Racism	aggressive behaviour towards (or treatment of) people who come from a different race by people who wish to be unkind and unfair to them
Recruit (employment)	find people and offer them work in a company or business
Redundant (employment)	no longer needed to do a particular job, e.g. if a person is made redundant, there is no longer a job for that person to do in a particular company and they will be asked to leave — if this happens the employee maybe entitled to receive an amount of money (redundancy pay)
Referendum	a vote by the public or by a governing body to decide on a course of action or to make a political decision
Refugees	people who must leave the country where they live often because of war or political reasons
Rent (housing)	pay to live in a room, flat or house that is owned by someone else
Report a crime	tell the police about an illegal action or activity
Residence	the place where someone lives their address

Restrict (immigration)	control and/or limit the number of people. e.g. a government might restrict the number of immigrants who can come and live in a country
Retire (employment)	stop going to work, usually at the age of 65 or older
Rise (in number, price)	increase, go up
Rival viewpoints	opinions that are held by different people or groups of people that are in opposition to each other
Roots (family)	the place that someone relates to because that was where s/he was born or where his/her family had their established home
Scratch card	a card that a person buys and then rubs with a coin to see if they have won money
Scrutinise	examine all the details
Seat (government)	a position that is officially held by someone in government who has been elected by the public and authorised to represent them
Secondary school	For children from age 11 (12 in Scotland), some are faith schools
Security	protection from something that could be dangerous, e.g. a person or thing that is secure is safe and protected from danger
Self-employed person	someone who works for themselves and not for an employer
Separation (family)	a situation where a married couple no longer live together but are not yet divorced
Serious misconduct (employment)	behaviour by someone in a job which is dishonest, bad or unprofessional, and because of which they may lose their job
Serious offences (law)	illegal actions or activities which are very bad and for which someone may have to go to prison for a long time, e.g. rape, murder
Shadow Cabinet	a group of senior MPs with special responsibilities who belong to a party that is not in government (which can also be called the opposition)
Sharia	loan for buying a house, and when the person who receives the loan only needs to pay back the original sum - no extra money needs to be paid
Sick pay	money received by an employee when s/he is unable to work because of illness
Social security	welfare benefits to people who do not have enough money to live on, for sick or disabled, older people, or unemployed and on low incomes
Solicitor	a professional person whose job is to give legal advice and prepare

	documents for legal procedures, e.g. divorce, buying and selling houses
Speaker, the	the person in government who controls the way issues are debated in Parliament
Standing order	an arrangement in which a bank or building society takes a fixed amount of money from one account and pays it into another account on a regular basis
Start-up loans	money given to someone to start up a new business that must be paid back with interest later
State pension	money paid regularly by the government to people who have retired from work, usually when they are 65 or older
Stepfamily	a family in which the mother or father is not the biological parent of one or more of the children, e.g. when a divorced woman re-marries, her new husband will be the stepfather to the children from her previous marriage
Surveyor (housing)	a person who examines a property (usually when it is for sale) and checks the condition of the building. S/he then writes an official report (a survey) which gives important information to the buyer about any problems, or about any repairs that might need to be done
Taxis	minicab — transport in which you pay a fare
Television	A device used for watching TV programmes and for which you must have a license
Tenancy	the period of time that a tenant rents a property from a landlord or landlady — often also relating to conditions about renting the property
Tenant	a person who pays money to a landlord to live in rented accommodation-a flat or a house
Terrorism	violence used by people who want to force governments to do something — the violence is usually random and unexpected so no one can feel really safe from it
Toddler (family)	small child, usually 1-2 years old-the age at which small children learn to walk
Trade union	an association of workers that protects its members' political rights
Training	the education, instruction, or discipline of a person or thing that is being trained
Trains	series of connected railroad cars pulled or pushed by one or more

	locomotives
Treaty	an official written agreement between countries or governments
Tuition fees	money paid to a teacher or to a school for being taught something
Unemployed	not doing a job and not getting any wages
University	an institution of learning of the highest level, having a college of liberal arts and a program of graduate studies together with several professional schools
Valid	legally acceptable, e.g. when someone wants to enter another country his/her passport must be valid for that to be allowed
Vehicle (transport)	something in which people can travel on the roads, e.g. a car or bus
Voluntary work	work which someone does because they want to and which they do for free, i.e. they do not receive any payment
Volunteer	someone who works for free or who offers to do something without payment
Wages (page)	an amount of money paid for work
War effort	the work that people did in order to support the country in whatever way they could during wartime
Welfare benefits	amounts of money paid by the government to people who have very little money of their own and who are perhaps unable to work or elderly or sick or disabled etc.
Withdraw (law)	step back from and stop taking part in a formal arrangement or activity
Withdraw (money)	take money out of an bank account or cash machine
Workforce	the group of people who work for a particular company or business or, on a larger scale, all the people who can work in a particular country or part of the world etc.
Yellow Pages	a book that lists names, addresses and telephone numbers of businesses, services and organisations in an area

Notes

Index

Life Peers, 50
local authorities
    local authority, *54*, *55*, *71*
Lord Chancellor, 51

M

magistrate, 56
mainland, 37
marital status, 34, 43, 136, 145
maternity leave, 120, 123
maternity services, 81, 85
media, 47, 57
mediation, 77
Member of Parliament, 48
mental illnesses
    mental illness, 80
meter
    housing, 74, 143
migrated, 21
misuse, 26, 27, 29
molestation, 24
monarch, 39, 43, 47, 65, 136
monarchy, 47
mortgage, 69, 70, 76, 142
MOT, 96
motor
    transport, 96
MP, 48, 49, 51, 52, 59, 136, 137, 144

N

National Curriculum, *27*, *88*, *89*
national insurance
    contributions, *115*

naturalised citizens, 57, 65
New Scotland Yard, 56
NHS
    National Health Service, 80, 83, 84, 99
Non-departmental public bodies, 56
not-for-profit, 71, 141
notice
    to give, 71, 109, 114, 118, 120, 123, 144
nuisance, 77, 99

O

occupation, 34, 43, 79
office
    to be in, 58
off-licence, 93, 99
online, 11, 111
on-the-spot fines, 26
Opposition, 51, 52, 53, 65, 144
Opticians, 85
Outpatient, 144
Outpatients
    outpatient, 84

P

party politics, 27
party system, 52
paternity leave, 120, 123
patient
    medical, 84, 142, 145
patron saint, 39
peers, 50
penalty

Notes

Order Form

You can place an order here for the companion publication Life in the UK Test Practice Questions for Citizenship & Settlement Tests. Over 1,000 revision questions and answers. A perfect study companion — all questions are based on the study materials published by the Home Office. Includes CD-ROM with an electronic version of our study guide, interactive practice test quizzes and helpful information.

You can also order from our website at www.lancasterandcoull.co.uk

Item	ISBN Number	Price	Qty	Total
Life in the UK Test Practice Questions for Citizenship (paperback)	978-0-9554853-4-3	£9.85		
Includes P&P				
		Total for order	£	

YOUR DETAILS

Name:	
Your reference number (if applicable)	
Address:	
Postcode:	
Telephone: Fax: Email:	

Please make cheques payable to LANCASTER AND COULL PUBLISHERS LTD. You can also do a direct bank deposit. Please contact us for our bank details.

Orders should be sent to: Order Department, 11 Milton Close, Horton, Berkshire SL3 9PP, United Kingdom

Email: orders@lancasterandcoull.co.uk   Website: www.lancasterandcoull.co.uk

Notes